M000106332

PRINT'S BEST LOGOS & SYMBOLS 3

Manufactured in Singapore

PRINT'S BEST LOGOS & SYMBOLS 3

Library of Congress Catalog Card Number 89-091068

ISBN 0-915734-85-0

RC PUBLICATIONS

President and Publisher: Howard Cadel

Vice President and Editor: Martin Fox

Creative Director: Andrew Kner

Managing Director, Book Projects: Linda Silver

Associate Art Director: Nell Coyle

Administrative Assistant: Nancy Silver

Print's Best
LOGOS & SYMBOLS

WINNING DESIGNS FROM PRINT MAGAZINE'S NATIONAL COMPETITION

Edited by

LINDA SILVER

Designed by

ANDREW KNER

Introduction by

STEVEN HELLER

Published by

RC PUBLICATIONS, INC.
NEW YORK, NY

Although the analogy might be a little off, design haiku is how I would describe the logos included in this volume. They are little gems of concept that say so much with so little; the best of them say it with wit and humor. Yet this was not always the case. Until fairly recently, the majority of business logos were pristine jewels in the crowns of corporate identity programs. Predominantly abstract, purportedly "universal," these marks of multinationalism exuded about as much warmth as the pure geometries from which they derived. Beginning around the mid-1950s, when the International Style promoted formal purity as an antidote to the naive sentimentalism of commercial art that had preceded it, the unadorned geometric logo was the model for all others to follow–the state of the art.

Logos began to evolve (or devolve) in the 1970s when it became clear that the International Style, though accepted throughout the world, was also producing clichés and redundancy that began to diminish effectiveness. AT&T's globe logo looked like Minolta's globe logo. NBC's million-dollar "N" was virtually the same as one owned by a local television station. By the '80s, computer-driven logo templates made it possible for any company to have its own geometric logo. The popularity of the purely objective device, once a radical alternative to trade characters and subjective marks, was on the wane. Today, a resurgence in the use of trade characters, visual puns, and other amiable symbols suggests that businesses–small and large–want to be seen as having a human face. Some seem to yearn to return to less complicated times by reviving old trade symbols. Even a high-tech company like Apple, on whose Mac this essay was written, has a warm and friendly logo/trademark to match its warm and friendly name.

This edition of *Print's Best Logos & Symbols* is a testament to the loosening, and humoring, up of logo design during

CONTENTS

the '90s. Some of these marks are nostalgic; some owe their inspiration to the sourcebooks of venerable trademarks published in the last decade. Others are virtual parodies of the International Style, borrowing on the geometric forms to create subjective images. And still others are unique concoctions that by serendipity or design hit the mark through clever invention. Most of them delightfully express the role of their particular businesses through graphic puzzles that are worth deciphering. Some are literal, but they are never mundane.

The graphic styles are diverse, too. While logos must be graphic, those represented here reveal a panoply of historical styles from Victorian to Postmodern. Doric columns are in abundance, as are Greek and Roman busts. Borrowing from the commercial art vernacular is apparent, but so is a classical simplicity. Compared to collections of logos and marks published even two decades ago, the carnival-like diversity of this contemporary assortment is dazzling.

Yet as lighthearted and easygoing as many of these specimens may be, the process of conceiving and designing them wasn't necessarily a lark. Combining just the visual right elements to create a meaningful symbol is no simple matter. Clichés are difficult things to avoid when doing a zoo logo or a dentist's mark. Not being cute is an even more difficult challenge. Yet miraculously, the vast majority of logos here have sidestepped the pitfalls. Instead, these logos represent a plateau of conceptual graphic design, a high level of thinking and skill.

These marks of the '90s attest to one fact: Ideology no longer governs the making of logos and symbols; circumstance does. The strictures are off and no idea is too ridiculous. The only standard is that they pique interest and be memorable, too.—*Steven Heller*

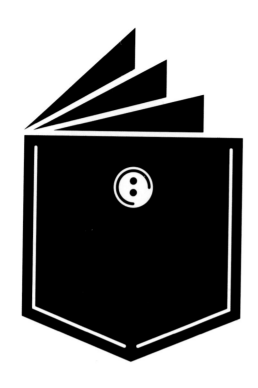

DESIGN FIRM:

Hornall Anderson Design

Works, Seattle, Washington

ART DIRECTOR:

Jack Anderson

DESIGNERS:

Jack Anderson, Julie

Tanagi-Lock, Mary Hermes,

Lian Ng

Jean Pierre Enterprises (Men's Fashion)

DESIGN FIRM:

Hirshorn-Zuckerman

Design, Rockville, Maryland

ART DIRECTOR/

DESIGNER/ILLUSTRATOR:

David Miller

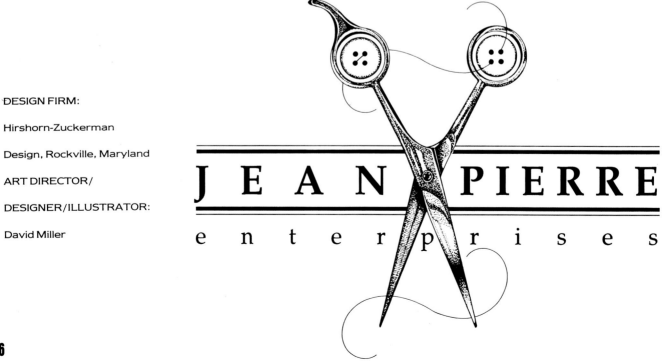

DESIGN FIRM:

Sommese Design, State

College, Pennsylvania

ART DIRECTOR/

DESIGNER:

Kristin Sommese

Europe's Fashion Finest

Boutique featuring women's

clothing from new European

designers.

DESIGN FIRM:

Bonapace Design, Astoria,

New York

ART DIRECTOR/

DESIGNER: Laura Bonapace

A school for gifted under-
privileged children.
DESIGN FIRM:
Malcolm Grear Designers,
Inc., Providence, Rhode
Island

Community Preparatory School

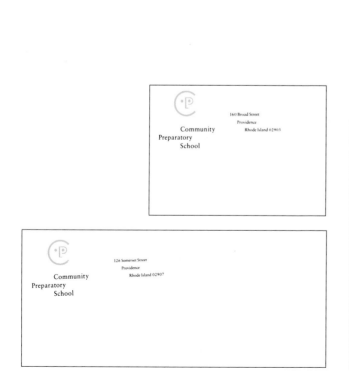

126 Somerset Street
Providence
Rhode Island 02907
401 521-9696

Community
Preparatory
School

160 Broad Street
Providence
Rhode Island 02903

Community
Preparatory
School

126 Somerset Street
Providence
Rhode Island 02907

Community
Preparatory
School

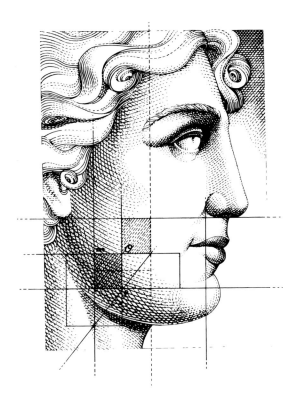

DESIGN FIRM:

Hornall Anderson Design

Works, Seattle, Washington

ART DIRECTOR:

Jack Anderson

DESIGNERS:

Jack Anderson, Brian

O'Neill, Lian Ng

ILLUSTRATOR: John Fretz

The Center for Oral and Maxillofacial Surgery

Fashion show fundraiser for

Pittsburgh animal shelters.

DESIGN FIRM:

Landesberg Design

Associates, Pittsburgh,

Pennsylvania

ART DIRECTORS:

Rick Landesberg, Mike

Savitski

DESIGNER/ILLUSTRATOR:

Mike Savitski

DESIGN FIRM: Moinx & Co.,

Auburn, Alabama

DESIGNER/ILLUSTRATOR:

Peter Spivak

Out of the Bag (Candy Manufacturer)

DESIGN FIRM:

Stewart, Tabori & Chang,

New York, New York

ART DIRECTOR/

DESIGNER: Jim Wageman

INKER: Tony DiSpigna

Stewart, Tabori & Chang (Publishing)

DESIGN FIRM: Pentagram,
New York, New York

ART DIRECTORS:
Colin Forbes, Michael Gericke

DESIGNERS:
Michael Gericke, Donna Ching

ILLUSTRATOR:
McRay Magleby

$$\begin{array}{c}\text{W O R L D W I D E} \\ \text{O P E R A T I O N S}\end{array}$$

$$\begin{array}{c}\text{M I S S I O N} \\ \text{S T A T E M E N T}\end{array}$$

$$\begin{array}{c}\text{S T R A T E G I C} \\ \text{I N I T I A T I V E S}\end{array}$$

V A L U E S

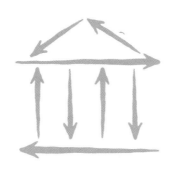

$$\begin{array}{c}\text{A R C H I T E C T U R A L} \\ \text{D I R E C T I O N}\end{array}$$

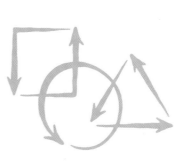

C O M P O N E N T S

DESIGN FIRM:

Earl Gee Design, San

Francisco, California

ART DIRECTOR/

ILLUSTRATOR: Earl Gee

DESIGNERS: Earl Gee,

Fani Chung

13

DESIGN FIRM: Pentagram,

New York, New York

ART DIRECTORS:

Colin Forbes, Michael Gericke

DESIGNER: Michael Gericke

ILLUSTRATOR: Mirko Ílic

Texas Biotechnology Corporation (Biotechnology)

DESIGN FIRM: Pentagram,

New York, New York

ART DIRECTORS:

Michael Gericke, Woody Pirtle

DESIGNERS:

Michael Gericke, Donna Ching

Apex Painting Company (Commercial Painting)

ART DIRECTOR/

DESIGNER/ILLUSTRATOR:

Jack Bollinger, Oregon, Ohio

Firehouse 101 Design

DESIGN FIRM:

Firehouse 101 Design,

Columbus, Ohio

DESIGNER/ILLUSTRATOR:

Kirk Richard Smith

TYPOGRAPHY:

Cardinal Type, Inc.

FIRE HOUSE 101

DESIGN

DESIGN FIRM:

Richards & Swensen, Inc.,

Salt Lake City, Utah

ART DIRECTOR/

DESIGNER:

Micheal Richards

DESIGNER:

William Swensen

Corporate symbol used for annual participation in the March of Dimes.

DESIGN FIRM:

Inter Ad Agency, Sarasota, Florida

DESIGNER: Peter Sliwinski

Annual polo match and
picnic fundraiser.
DESIGN FIRM:
Wenz-Neely Company,
Louisville, Kentucky
ART DIRECTOR/
DESIGNER/ILLUSTRATOR:
Phillip Booth

Prosthetic Research Foundation (Artificial Limbs)

DESIGN FIRM:
Greg Welsh Design, Seattle,
Washington
ART DIRECTOR/
DESIGNER/ILLUSTRATOR:
Greg Welsh

Corporate ride-share program for commuters.
AGENCY:
Saatchi & Saatchi DFS/ Pacific, Torrance, California
ASSOCIATE CREATIVE DIRECTOR:
Dean Van Eimeren
DESIGNER/ILLUSTRATOR:
Karen Knecht

Saatchi & Saatchi DFS/Pacific (Advertising)

286 flatbush ave.

brooklyn, new york 11217

tel. 718·638·0550

fax 718·773·9869

DESIGN FIRM:

Robert Padovano Design,

Brooklyn, New York

ART DIRECTOR/

DESIGNER:

Robert Padovano

Music Emporium (Music/Record Store)

Designation for the music

area at a children's outdoor,

multi-activity festival.

DESIGN FIRM:

Lambert Design Studio,

Dallas, Texas

ART DIRECTOR:

Christie Lambert

DESIGNER/ILLUSTRATOR:

Joy Cathey

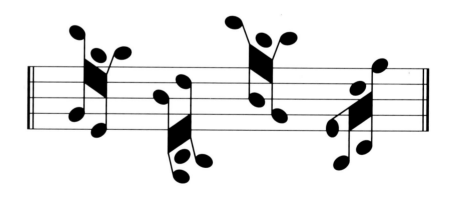

Kids' Music

DESIGN FIRM:

Hawley Martin Partners,

Richmond, Virginia

ART DIRECTOR/

ILLUSTRATOR: Doug Malott

In Your Ear Music & Recording Services

DESIGN FIRM:

Evans/Salt Lake, Salt Lake

City, Utah

ART DIRECTOR/

DESIGNER/ILLUSTRATOR:

Jeff Olsen

ALPINE SCHOOL DISTRICT

Alpine School District (Education)

Symbol for marketing
program for small
businesses.
AGENCY:
Nancy Gagne Graphic Design,
Boxford, Massachusetts
ART DIRECTOR/
DESIGNER/ILLUSTRATOR:
Nancy K. Gagne

 Institute for Media Arts

Institute for Media Arts (Filmmaking)

Organization that
encourages minority
filmmakers.
DESIGN FIRM:
Jon Wells Associates, San
Francisco, California
ART DIRECTOR/
DESIGNER/ILLUSTRATOR:
Jon Wells

CANADA

Canadian section logo of

Clairol's quarterly newsletter.

DESIGN FIRM:

Mike Quon Design Office,

New York, New York

ART DIRECTOR:

Scott Fishoff

DESIGNERS:

Eileen Kinneary, Mike Quon

ILLUSTRATOR: Mike Quon

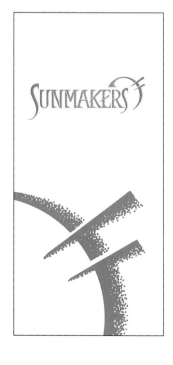

VIP LUGGAGE

NAME

ADDRESS IN U.S.

CITY

STATE   ZIP

DESTINATION CITY

HOTEL

DESIGN FIRM:

Hornall Anderson Design

Works, Seattle, Washington

ART DIRECTOR/DESIGNER:

Jani Drewfs

DESIGNER: John Hornall

ILLUSTRATOR: Dia Calhoun

DESIGN FIRM:

Mark Mock Design

Associates Inc., Denver,

Colorado

ART DIRECTOR: Mark Mock

DESIGNER: Jennifer Gilliland

Hawaiian travel incentive

program.

DESIGN FIRM:

Mires Design, Inc., San

Diego, California

ART DIRECTOR/DESIGNER:

Scott Mires

ILLUSTRATOR: Tracy Sabin

DESIGNER/ILLUSTRATOR:

Nancy Stentz, Seattle,

Washington

DESIGN FIRM:

Advertising Associates

ART DIRECTOR: Jim Ault

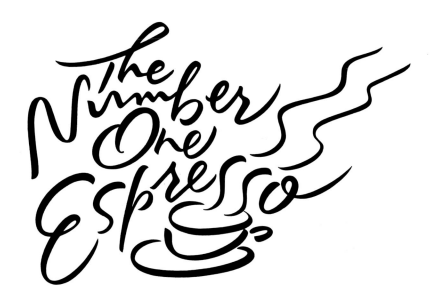

DESIGN FIRM:

Grafik Communications, Ltd.,

Alexandria, Virginia

ART DIRECTOR:

Susan English

DESIGNER: Michael Shea

Racheli's (Espresso Bar)

DESIGN FIRM: Tharp Did It,

Los Gatos, California

DESIGNER: Rick Tharp

ILLUSTRATORS:

Jean Mogannam, Jana Heer

LETTERER: Kim Tomlinson

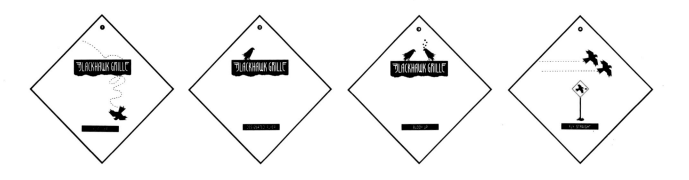

Marsh Restaurant

DESIGN FIRM:

Design Center, Minnetonka,

Minnesota

ART DIRECTOR: John Reger

DESIGNER: Kobe

DESIGN FIRM:

Tim Girvin Design, Inc.,

Seattle, Washington

ART DIRECTOR: Tim Girvin

SENIOR GRAPHIC

DESIGNER:

Stephen Pannone (menu)

DESIGNER: Tim Girvin (logo)

ILLUSTRATOR: Tim Girvin

(menu)

Gourmet Gardens (Restaurant)

DESIGN FIRM:

Woods & Woods, San

Francisco, California

ART DIRECTOR/

DESIGNER/ILLUSTRATOR:

Paul Woods

GOURMET
GARDENS

Association of business and
property owners in historic
urban area of Richmond.

DESIGN FIRM:

Stygar Group, Inc.,

Richmond, Virginia

ART DIRECTOR/DESIGNER:

James A. Stygar

DESIGN FIRM:

Chameleon Design,

Phoenix, Arizona

ART DIRECTOR:

Curt Prickett

DESIGNERS: Curt Prickett,

Tina Owyung

PACK OF LIES

Logo for anti-smoking

 program.

DESIGN FIRM:

Peterson & Company,

Dallas, Texas

ART DIRECTOR/DESIGNER:

Scott Paramski

Knockout Signs & Banners

DESIGN FIRM:

Jane Gerke Design, Mesa,

Arizona

ART DIRECTOR/

DESIGNER/ILLUSTRATOR:

Jane Gerke

Heffron Design Team

DESIGN FIRM:

Chameleon Design,

Phoenix, Arizona

ART DIRECTOR/DESIGNER:

Cindy Jennings

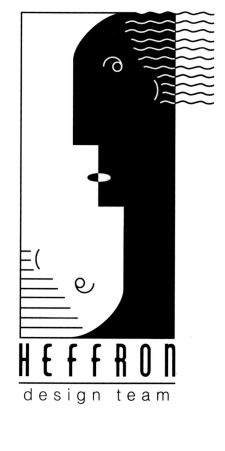

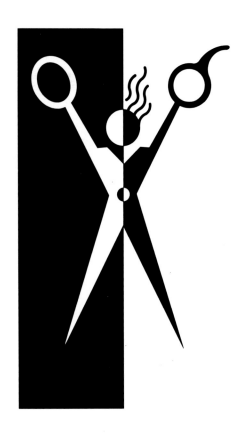

Becky Cutter (Hair Stylist)

DESIGN FIRM:

Graphics Network, Long

Beach, California

ART DIRECTOR/DESIGNER:

Tom Cutter

DESIGN FIRM:

Thomas Design, Santa

Clara, California

DESIGNER: Craig Thomas

Arizona Public Service Company

Logo for electric utility's

annual conference on

women's issues.

DESIGN FIRM:

Arizona Public Service Co.,

Phoenix, Arizona

DESIGNER:

Karen Daugherty

Logo for annual orientation retreat for new students.

DESIGN FIRM:

Dean Wilhite Design Company, Oklahoma City, Oklahoma

ART DIRECTOR/ DESIGNER/ILLUSTRATOR:

Dean Wilhite

A Z U S A   P A C I F I C   U N I V E R S I T Y

Western Star Designs (Western Jewelry Designer/Maker)

DESIGN FIRM:

Palmquist & Palmquist Design, Bozeman, Montana

ART DIRECTORS/ DESIGNERS:

Kurt and Denise Palmquist

ILLUSTRATOR:

Kurt Palmquist

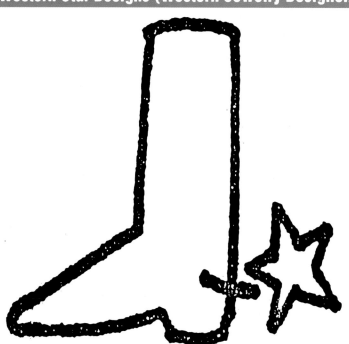

DESIGN FIRM:

Morreal Graphic Design,

San Diego, California

DESIGNER/ILLUSTRATOR:

Mary Lou Morreal

Annual film festival symbol.

ART DIRECTOR/DESIGNER:

Dung Hoang, Salt Lake

City, Utah

Asian Association of Utah

33

Sandra Sabo (Writer/Editor)

DESIGN FIRM:

Supon Design Group, Inc.,

Washington, DC

ART DIRECTOR:

Supon Phornirunlit

DESIGNER: Dave Prescott

Education fund symbol.

DESIGN FIRM: Fritts &

Hanna, Erie, Pennsylvania

ART DIRECTOR: Gary Fritts

DESIGNER: Dawn Bishop

Diocese of Erie (Religious Education)

DESIGN FIRM:

Tocquigny Design, Inc.,

Austin, Texas

ART DIRECTOR:

Yvonne Tocquigny

DESIGNER: Scott Herron

ACCOUNT SERVICE:

Sherry Smith

Dr. Leonard Tom D.D.S. & Associates (Dentistry)

Ginny's Printing & Copying

DESIGN FIRM:

Barrett Design, Inc.,

Cambridge, Massachusetts

ART DIRECTOR:

Karen Dendy

DESIGNERS: Karen Dendy,

Rob Keohane

DESIGN FIRM:

Bruce E. Morgan Graphic

Design, Washington, DC

ART DIRECTOR/DESIGNER:

Bruce E. Morgan

Caesar's Tropical Fish

DESIGN FIRM:

Glenn Martinez & Associates,

Santa Rosa, California

ART DIRECTOR:

Kathleen Nelson

DESIGNER: Glenn Martinez

DESIGN FIRM:

Campbell Fisher Ditko

Design, Phoenix, Arizona

ART DIRECTOR/DESIGNER:

Steve Ditko

ILLUSTRATOR: John Kleber

DESIGN FIRM:

Donald E. Smolen &

Associates, Los Angeles,

California

ART DIRECTOR:

Donald E. Smolen

DESIGNER:

J. Robert Faulkner

PRODUCTION DESIGN:

Michelle Park

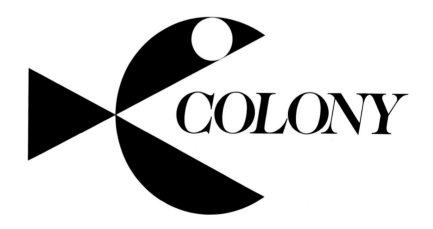

Colony Pictures (Filmmaking)

DESIGN FIRM:

Introspective Design,

Cincinnati, Ohio

ART DIRECTOR/DESIGNER:

Michael Todd Lott

Holtel Construction

Club logo for college
students involved in
literature, fine arts, music
and theater.

ART DIRECTOR/
DESIGNER/ILLUSTRATOR:
Peter E. Horjus, San Diego,
California

Point Loma College (Education)

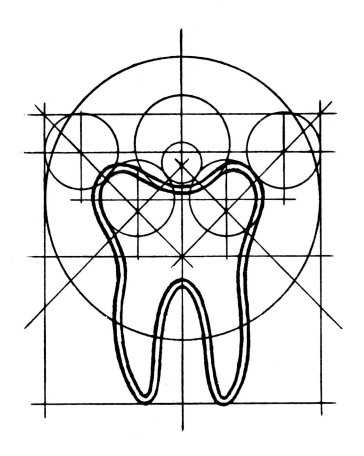

DESIGN FIRM:

Rhino Graphics, Webster,

New York

ART DIRECTOR:

Robert Kiesow

DESIGNERS:

Robert Kiesow, Joe Oster

DESIGN FIRM:

Sawcheese Studio, Santa

Monica, California

ART DIRECTOR/

DESIGNER/ILLUSTRATOR:

Sachi Kuwahara

Pronto Pollo (Fast-Food Restaurant)

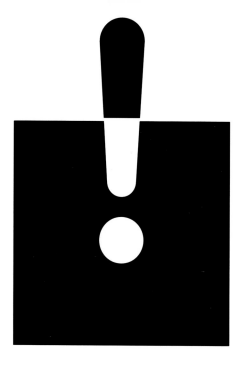

DESIGN FIRM: Studio A,

Alexandria, Virginia

ART DIRECTOR/DESIGNER:

Antonio Alcala

Uncommon Sense Consulting (Computer Consulting)

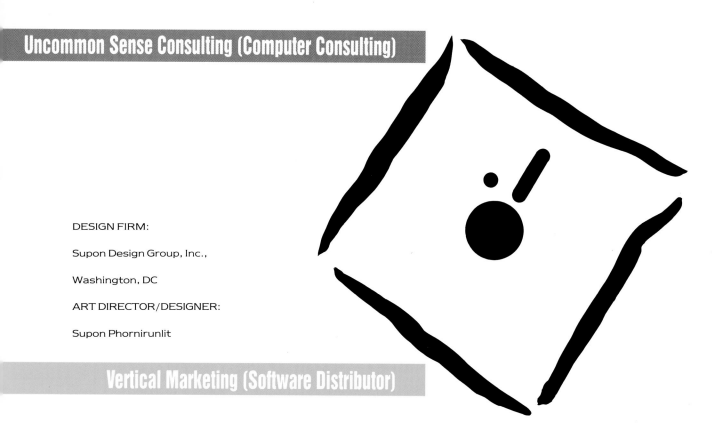

DESIGN FIRM:

Supon Design Group, Inc.,

Washington, DC

ART DIRECTOR/DESIGNER:

Supon Phornirunlit

Vertical Marketing (Software Distributor)

DESIGN FIRM:

Robert Rigel Design,

Olympia, Washington

ART DIRECTOR/

DESIGNER/ILLUSTRATOR:

Robert Rigel

Robert Rigel Design

Work rehabilitation

program symbol.

DESIGN FIRM:

Bennett Peji Design, San

Diego, California

ART DIRECTORS:

Bennett Peji, Lynn Scott

DESIGNER/ILLUSTRATOR:

Bennett Peji

Scripps Clinic & Research Foundation (Health Care)

Series of logos announcing

the addition of evening

dining hours.

DESIGN FIRM:

Kirby Stephens Design, Inc.,

Somerset, Kentucky

ART DIRECTOR:

Kirby Stephens

DESIGNER: Bill Jones

DESIGN FIRM:

Rusty Kay & Associates,

Santa Monica, California

ART DIRECTOR: Rusty Kay

DESIGNER/ILLUSTRATOR:

Susan Rogers

w o r l d   c a f e

Goodies Inc.

Gift shop logos at Children's

Hospital in Boston.

DESIGN FIRM:

DiSanto Design, Boston,

Massachusetts

DESIGNER/ILLUSTRATOR:

Rose DiSanto

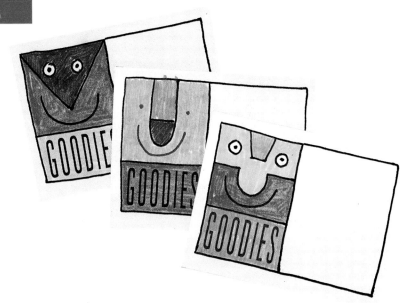

Charitable organization that unites children through baseball.

DESIGN FIRM:

Shimokochi/Reeves, Los Angeles, California

ART DIRECTORS:

Mamoru Shimokochi, Anne Reeves

DESIGNER:

Mamoru Shimokochi

World Children's Baseball Fair

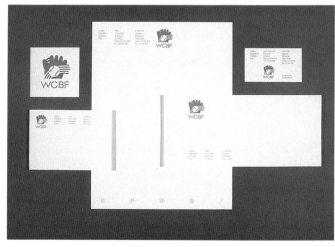

Tokyo Broadcasting System

DESIGN FIRM:

Shimokochi/Reeves, Los

Angeles, California

ART DIRECTORS:

Mamoru Shimokochi, Anne

Reeves

DESIGNER:

Mamoru Shimokochi

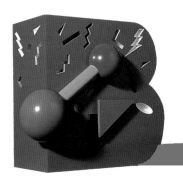

Tokyo Broadcasting System (Television Network)

Logo for a walking tour of quilts held each year in Bell Buckle, Tennessee.

DESIGN FIRM: Ellis Design, Nashville, Tennessee

ART DIRECTORS/ DESIGNERS:

Jan and Laurie Ellis

DESIGN FIRM:

Milton Glaser, Inc., New York, New York

ART DIRECTOR/DESIGNER:

Milton Glaser

Queens College

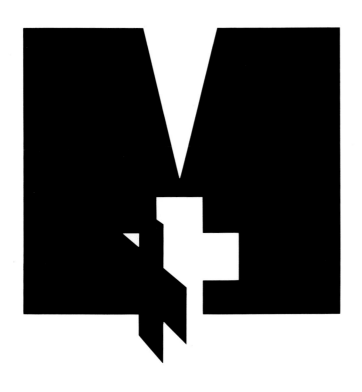

A system providing
consumers with access to
medical information.

DESIGN FIRM:
Brinkley & Izard Design and
Advertising, Charlotte,
North Carolina

ART DIRECTOR: Kathy Izard

DESIGNER: Leigh Brinkley

ILLUSTRATORS:
Leigh Brinkley, Greg Ridge

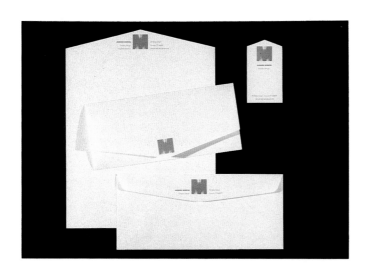

Minoru Morita

DESIGNER: Minoru Morita,
Cos Cob, Connecticut

47

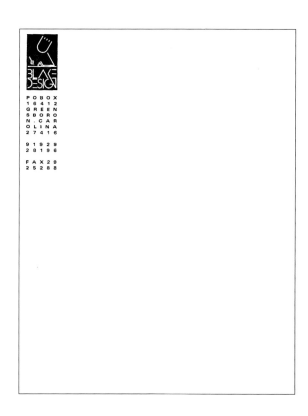

DESIGN FIRM:

Blake Design, Greensboro,

North Carolina

ART DIRECTOR/DESIGNER:

Tim Blake

P O B O X
1 6 4 1 2
G R E E N
S B O R O
N . C A R
O L I N A
2 7 4 1 6

Blake Design

American Medical Videos, Inc.

Producer of instructional

videos for doctors and their

patients.

DESIGN FIRM: Ford Design,

Marietta, Georgia

ART DIRECTOR/

ILLUSTRATOR: Craig Ford

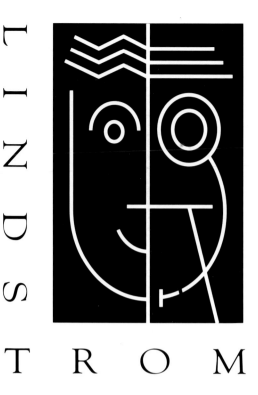

L
I
N
D
S
T   R   O   M

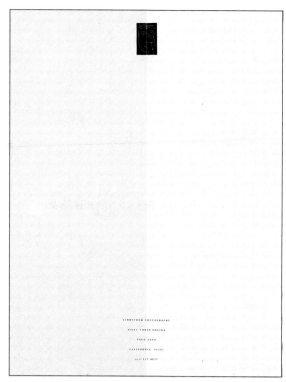

DESIGN FIRM:

Lauren Smith Design, Palo

Alto, California

DESIGNER/ILLUSTRATOR:

Lauren Smith

Lindstrom Photography

Steven Marylander Wines (Vineyard)

DESIGN FIRM:

Bruce Yelaska Design,

San Francisco, California

ART DIRECTOR/

DESIGNER/ILLUSTRATOR:

Bruce Yelaska

DESIGN FIRM:

Mark Palmer Design, Palm

Desert, California

ART DIRECTOR:

Mark Palmer

DESIGNERS: Mark Palmer,

Pat Kellogg

Cactus Café

PRICKLY PEAR
S T U D I O

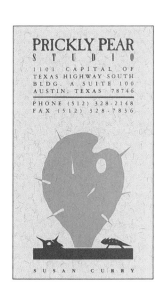

DESIGN FIRM:

Prickly Pear Studio, Austin,

Texas

ART DIRECTOR/

ILLUSTRATOR: Tom Curry

DESIGNERS:

Susan and Tom Curry

Prickly Pear Studio

DESIGN FIRM:

Pennebaker Design,

Houston, Texas

ART DIRECTOR/DESIGNER:

David Lerch

Dancing Desert Press (Publishing)

DESIGN FIRM:

Vaughn/Wedeen Creative,

Albuquerque, New Mexico

ART DIRECTOR/

DESIGNER/ILLUSTRATOR:

Rick Vaughn

DESIGN FIRM:

ADS/Graphics, Boone,

North Carolina

ART DIRECTOR:

Dana Willett

DESIGNERS: Dana Willett,

Carol Aldridge

ILLUSTRATOR:

Carol Aldridge

Cheap Joes Art Stuff (Art Supply Store)

Annual bike-a-thon for a

group theater.

DESIGN FIRM: Modern Dog,

Seattle, Washington

ART DIRECTORS:

Laura Newton, Vittorio

Costarella

DESIGNER:

Vittorio Costarella

Seattle Group Theatre

DESIGN FIRM:

Joe Rattan Design, Dallas,

Texas

ART DIRECTOR/DESIGNER:

Alan Colvin

AGENCY:

Young & Laramore,

Indianapolis, Indiana

CREATIVE DIRECTORS:

David Young, Jeff Laramore

ART DIRECTOR:

Jeff Laramore

ILLUSTRATOR:

Scott Montgomery

Chatterbox (Jazz Bar)

DESIGN FIRM:

Bob Coonts Design Group,

Ft. Collins, Colorado

ART DIRECTOR: Bob Coonts

DESIGNER: Anne Vetter

Logo for an arts and

ecucation program that

teaches academic subjects

through art.

DESIGN FIRM:

Maureen Erbe Design, Los

Angeles, California

ART DIRECTOR:

Maureen Erbe

DESIGNERS:

Maureen Erbe, Rita A.

Sowins

ARTSOURCE

Krawczyk Design, Inc.

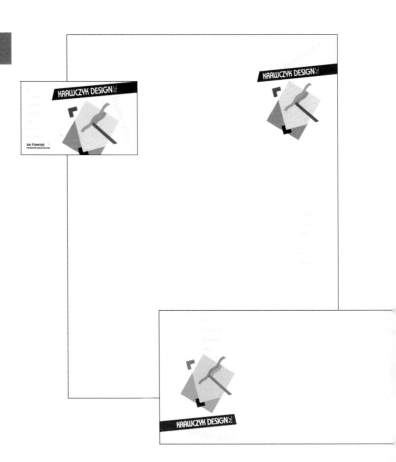

DESIGN FIRM:

Krawczyk Design, Inc.,

Orlando, Florida

DESIGNER: Joe Krawczyk

Dung Hoang (Designer)

ART DIRECTOR/DESIGNER:

Dung Hoang, Salt Lake City,

Utah

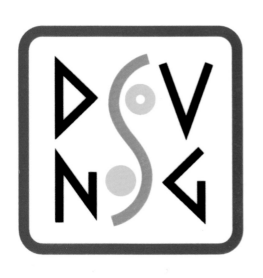

OrlandoHumaneSociety

AGENCY: Cramer Krasselt,

Orlando, Florida

ART DIRECTOR: Mitch Boyd

Orlando Humane Society

DESIGN FIRM:

Sibley/Peteet Design,

Dallas, Texas

ART DIRECTORS:

David Beck, Rex Peteet

DESIGNER/ILLUSTRATOR:

David Beck

Los Arcos Mall Shuttle Service

56

Public relations division of
an advertising agency.

DESIGN FIRM:

O'Keefe Marketing,

Richmond, Virginia

ART DIRECTOR/DESIGNER:

Kelly O'Keefe

ILLUSTRATOR:

Scott Wright

Arizona Heritage Alliance

A public agency using lottery
money for historical, land,
and wildlife preservation.

ART DIRECTOR/DESIGNER:

Karen Daugherty/Arizona
Public Service Co., Phoenix,
Arizona

Symbol for Eye/Vision
Program.
DESIGN FIRM:
Michael Gerbino Designs,
Inc., New York, New York
ART DIRECTOR:
Michael Gerbino
DESIGNER: Niko Courtelis

The International Environmental Film Festival

Festival in Boulder that
promotes environmental
awareness through film.
DESIGN FIRM:
Merten Design Group,
Denver, Colorado
ART DIRECTOR:
Barry A. Merten
DESIGNER/ILLUSTRATOR:
Kathy Thompson

DESIGN FIRM:

Kuo Design Group,

New York, New York

ART DIRECTOR/DESIGNER:

Samuel Kuo

DESIGN FIRM: Image

Design, Inc., Nashville,

Tennessee

DESIGNER: Robert Froedge

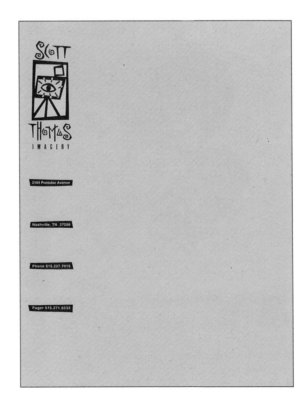

2104 Pontotoc Avenue

Nashville, TN 37206

Phone 615.227.7015

Pager 615.271.6533

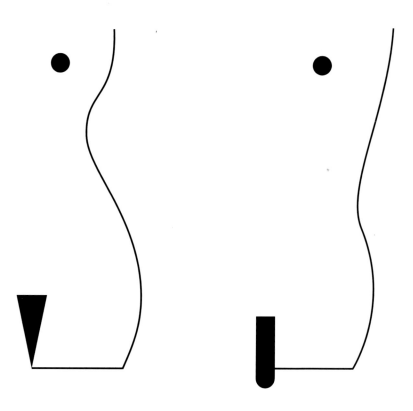

Restroom signs.

DESIGN FIRM: Wood Design,

New York, New York

DESIGNER/ILLUSTRATOR:

Tom Wood

Wood Design

DESIGN FIRM:

Hull & Honeycutt,

Sacramento, California

ART DIRECTOR: Susan Hull

DESIGNER/ILLUSTRATOR:

Annette Mirviss

Solano Family Physicians (Healthcare)

Renee Comet Photography

DESIGN FIRM:

Bruce E. Morgan Graphic

Design, Washington, DC

ART DIRECTOR/DESIGNER:

Bruce E. Morgan

BRUCE COLEMAN

PHOTO LIBRARY

DESIGN FIRM:

Edward Walter Design,

New York, New York

ART DIRECTOR/DESIGNER:

Edward Walter

Bruce Coleman, Inc. (Photo Library)

DESIGN FIRM:

Simon & Cirulis, St. Louis,

Missouri

ART DIRECTOR/DESIGNER:

Frank Roth

ILLUSTRATOR: Jim Roth

BRITH
SHOLOM
KNESETH
ISRAEL

DESIGN FIRM:

Dale Vermeer Design,

Honolulu, Hawaii

ART DIRECTOR/DESIGNER:

Dale Vermeer

Reimann Mikami (Furniture Design)

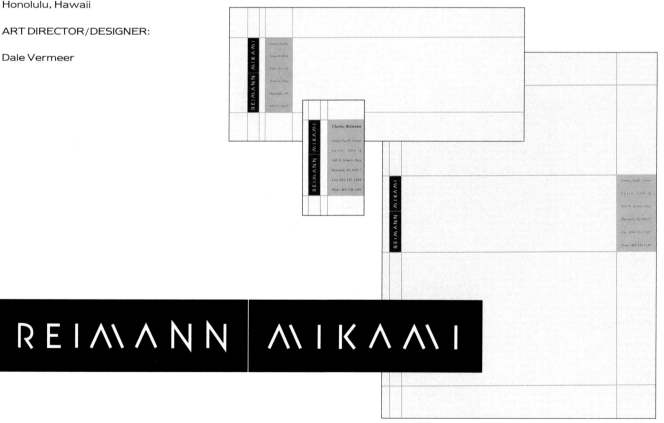

REIMANN MIKAMI

ASMT

DESIGN FIRM:

Pensaré Design Group Ltd.,

Washington, DC

ART DIRECTOR:

Mary Ellen Vehlow

DESIGNER: Diane Philmlee

ART DIRECTOR:

Nicholas Sinadinos,

Chicago, Illinois

DESIGNERS:

Nicholas Sinadinos,

Hiromi Takahashi

Astro Kids (Children's Clothing Store)

DESIGN FIRM:

Dog Eat Dog Productions,

Stone Mountain, Georgia

ART DIRECTOR/

DESIGNER/ILLUSTRATOR:

Jerry Silvestrini

Dog Eat Dog Productions (Illustration Studio)

Good Dog / Bad Dog

DESIGN FIRM:

Sandstrom Design, Inc.,

Portland, Oregon

DESIGNER/ILLUSTRATOR:

Kurt Holloman

Good Dog/Bad Dog (Restaurant)

Manufacturer of clothing for ages 12-30.
ART DIRECTOR/DESIGNER:
Joseph Tomko, Pittsburgh, Pennsylvania
ILLUSTRATOR:
Burton Morris

DESIGNER/ILLUSTRATOR:
Stephen Schudlich, Troy, Michigan
AGENCY: W.B. Doner
ART DIRECTOR: Amy Swita

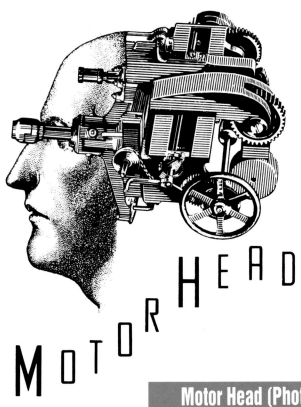

M O T O R H E A D

ART DIRECTORS/

DESIGNERS/

ILLUSTRATORS:

Mary Cawein, Louisville,

Kentucky; Walter McCord

Motor Head (Photography)

Producer of custom storage

drawers that drop down

from the ceiling.

ART DIRECTOR/DESIGNER:

Caroline Misner, Los

Angeles, California

Dropping Drawers

AGENCY:

Slaughter Hanson

Advertising, Birmingham,

Alabama

ART DIRECTOR/

ILLUSTRATOR:

Maya S. Metz

DESIGNER: Terry Slaughter

Volunteer support group.

DESIGN FIRM:

Sullivan Perkins, Dallas,

Texas

ART DIRECTOR:

Ron Sullivan

DESIGNER/ILLUSTRATOR:

Art Garcia

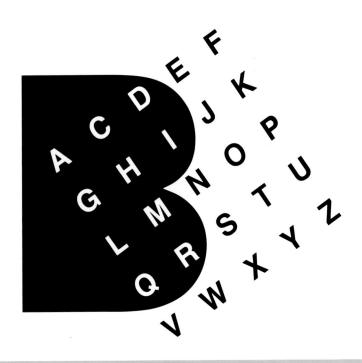

Logo for a corporate

spelling bee.

DESIGN FIRM:

Vance Wright Adams &

Associates, Pittsburgh,

Pennsylvania

ART DIRECTOR:

Gary Adams

DESIGNER: Susan Boroch

Ketchum Public Relations

Company involved in the

research and development

of environmentally

responsible cleaning

products.

DESIGN FIRM:

Vance Wright Adams &

Associates, Pittsburgh,

Pennsylvania

ART DIRECTOR:

Tarmo Vance

DESIGNER: Susan Boroch

CleanQuest

Financial services provided

via the telephone.

DESIGN FIRM:

Eisenberg & Associates,

Dallas, Texas

CREATIVE DIRECTOR:

Arthur Eisenberg

ART DIRECTORS:

Raul Varela, Bruce Wynne

Jones

DESIGNER/ILLUSTRATOR:

Raul Varela

DESIGN FIRM:

Williams McBride Design,

Lexington, Kentucky

ART DIRECTORS:

Jim Wilmink, Robin Williams

Brohm

DESIGNER: Jim Wilmink

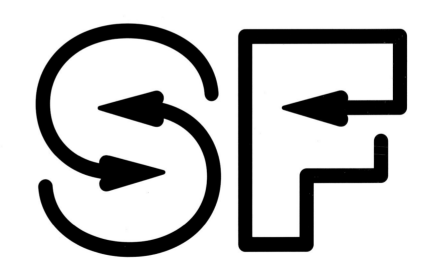

Staggs & Fisher (Mechanical and Electrical Engineers)

Symbol for annual

fundraiser.

DESIGN FIRM:

Harrisberger Creative,

Virginia Beach, Virginia

ART DIRECTOR/

DESIGNER/ILLUSTRATOR:

Lynn Harrisberger

KUBU Communications (Graphic Design)

DESIGN FIRM:

Pearlman & Partners,

Darien, Connecticut

DESIGNER: Robert

Pearlman

Kubu Communications
3356 Noroton Station
Darien, CT 06820
Fone: 203.656.2087
Fax: 203.656.0475

Gira Polli (Restaurant)

DESIGN FIRM:

Melanie Doherty Design,

San Francisco, California

ART DIRECTOR:

Melanie Doherty

DESIGNERS:

Melanie Doherty, Joan

Folkmann

Merchandising symbol.

DESIGN FIRM:

Parham-Santana Inc., New

York, New York

ART DIRECTOR/

DESIGNER/ILLUSTRATOR:

Rick Tesoro

New York Zoological Society

ART DIRECTOR:

Peter Winecke,

Minneapolis, Minneapolis

DESIGNERS: Peter Winecke,

Jim Marson

ART DIRECTOR/

DESIGNER/ILLUSTRATOR:

David Grandin, Danville,

California

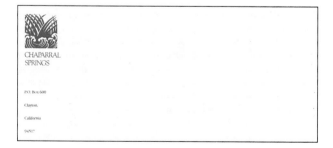

CHAPARRAL
SPRINGS

P.O. Box 600

Clayton,

California

94517

72

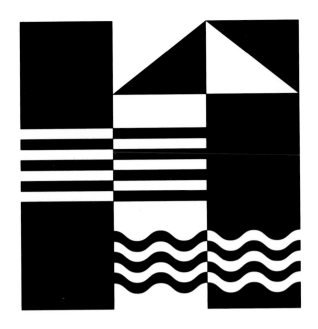

Symbol for corporate headquarters project.

ART DIRECTOR:
Fred Murrell/Corning

Corporate Design, Corning, New York

DESIGNERS: Brian Jones, Bill Lucas

Corning, Inc.

DESIGN FIRM:
Krawczyk Design, Inc., Orlando, Florida

DESIGNER: Joe Krawczyk

Pine Harbor Point Homeowners' Association

Interactive movement

center for children ages 3-6.

AGENCY: Siri Nadler Design,

Elkins Park, Pennsylvania

ART DIRECTOR:

Alice Dreuding

DESIGNER/ILLUSTRATOR:

Siri Nadler

Moving Studios

MOVING·STUDIOS

DANCE·STATIO

DESIGN FIRM:

A Houston Advertising,

Atlanta, Georgia

DESIGNER/ILLUSTRATOR:

Ann Houston

CALLIGRAPHER:

Joey Hannaford

PRODUCTION:

Holly Crispens

Logo for an environmental

club developed by the shop

whose focus is on recycling.

DESIGN FIRM:

Garma Graphic Design, Inc.,

Waipahu, Hawaii

ART DIRECTOR/DESIGNER:

Alfredo Lista Garma

ILLUSTRATOR: Leo Elaydo

Summer's Place (Novelty/Gift Shop)

ART DIRECTOR/DESIGNER:

Elizabeth Hoffman Gabel,

Rochester, New York

DESIGN FIRM: Modern Dog,

Seattle, Washington

ART DIRECTORS:

Arthur Strom, Michael

Strassburger

DESIGN DIRECTOR/

ILLUSTRATOR:

Michael Strassburger

American Design & Manufacturing

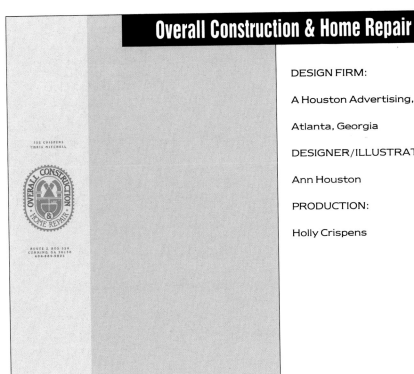

DESIGN FIRM:

A Houston Advertising,

Atlanta, Georgia

DESIGNER/ILLUSTRATOR:

Ann Houston

PRODUCTION:

Holly Crispens

DESIGN FIRM: Cornerstone,

Baltimore, Maryland

ART DIRECTOR/DESIGNER:

Gerry Frank

ILLUSTRATOR: Jack Hovey

Linda's Custom Sewing

Fundraiser symbol for a new
school for developmentally
delayed children.

DESIGN FIRM:

Susanna Ronner Graphic

Design, Bearsville,

New York

DESIGNER/ILLUSTRATOR:

Susanna Ronner

PHOTOGRAPHER: Will Faller

Wildwood School

A Campaign for Wildwood School

FOR ONCE IN A LIFETIME

Non-profit organization that brings together inner-city children (from Hell's Kitchen) and professional artists to produce theater.

DESIGN FIRM:
The 52nd Street Project, New York, New York

ART DIRECTORS:
Iris A. Brown, Willie Reale

DESIGNERS: Iris A. Brown, Shel Silverstein

ILLUSTRATOR:
Shel Silverstein

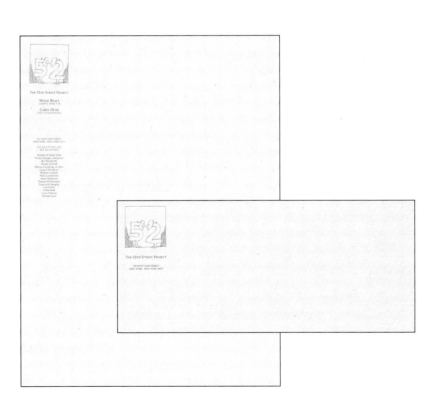

SUPON DESIGN GROUP, INC.

INTERNATIONAL BOOK DIVISION

1000 CONNECTICUT AVE. NW

SUITE FOUR HUNDRED FIFTEEN

WASHINGTON, DC 20036

Symbol for the international

book division of a graphic

design firm.

DESIGN FIRM:

Supon Design Group, Inc.,

Washington, DC

ART DIRECTOR:

Supon Phornirunlit

DESIGNERS: Dave Prescott

(symbol), Dianne Cook

(stationery)

Logo for a spring clean-up

campaign.

DESIGN FIRM:

Pennebaker Design,

Houston, Texas

ART DIRECTORS:

Ward Pennebaker, Jeffrey

McKay

DESIGNER: Jeffrey McKay

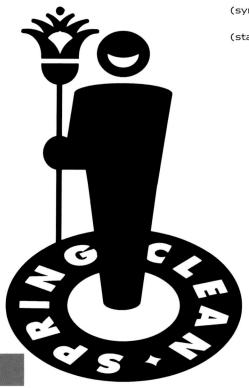

Hoechst Celanese (Chemical)

Logo for a program of public artworks and performances to promote the Market Street transit system.

DESIGN FIRM:

Earl Gee Design, San Francisco, California

ART DIRECTOR/ ILLUSTRATOR: Earl Gee

DESIGNERS: Earl Gee, Fani Chung

Personal stationery for an avid golfer.

DESIGN FIRM:

Sayles Graphic Design, Inc., Des Moines , Iowa

ART DIRECTOR/DESIGNER:

John Sayles

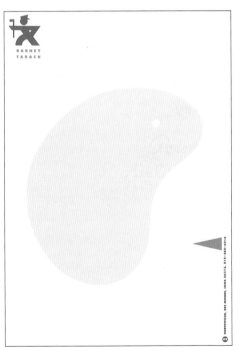

Barney Tabach

BARNEY TABACH

g

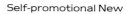

Self-promotional New Year's greeting.
DESIGN FIRM: Pictogram Studio, Washington, DC
ART DIRECTOR/ILLUSTRATOR: Hien Nguyen
DESIGNERS: Hien Nguyen, Stephanie Hooton

Pictogram Studio

DESIGN FIRM:

Pictogram Studio,

Washington, DC

DESIGNER:

Stephanie Hooton

ILLUSTRATOR:

Hien Nguyen

The Women & Children's Center of Fairfax Hospital

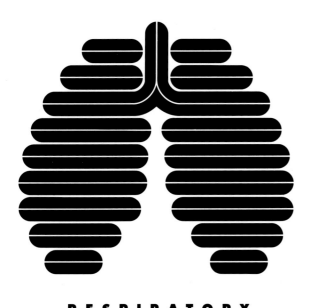

**R E S P I R A T O R Y
T E A M**

Team of researchers and
patients working to find
cures for lung disorders.
DESIGN FIRM: Glaxo, Inc.,
Research Triangle Park,
North Carolina
CREATIVE DIRECTOR:
Chig Wills
ART DIRECTOR:
Holly Russell
DESIGNER/ILLUSTRATOR:
Paul Barth

DESIGN FIRM:

Harrisberger Creative,

Virginia Beach, Virginia

ART DIRECTOR/

DESIGNER/ILLUSTRATOR:

Lynn Harrisberger

Pahnke, Charney Chiropractic

ART DIRECTOR/DESIGNER:

Rudi Backart, River Forest,

Illinois

PRINTER:

Nu-tone Printing Company

ENGRAVER:

Fine Arts Engraving

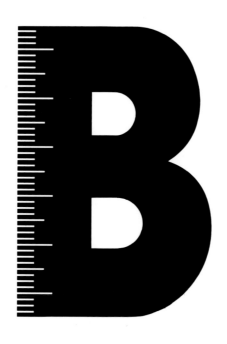

DESIGN FIRM:

Janet Hughes and

Associates, Wilmington,

Delaware

CREATIVE DIRECTOR:

Donna Perzel

ART DIRECTOR/DESIGNER:

Paul Di Campli

ACCOUNT SUPERVISOR:

Janet Hughes

Bancroft Construction Company

DESIGN FIRM:

Planet Design Company,

Madison , Wisconsin

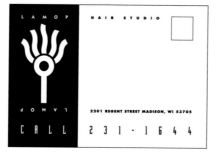

Twigs Restaurant

AGENCY: Crispin & Porter

Advertising, Miami, Florida

ART DIRECTOR/

DESIGNER: Alex Bogusky

T W I G S

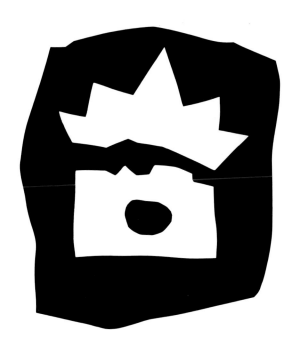

DESIGN FIRM:

Malowany.Chiocchi.Design,

Boulder, Colorado

ART DIRECTOR:

Gene Malowany

DESIGNER: Tim Fisher

David H. Ramsey (Photographer)

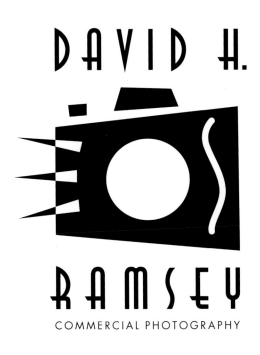

DESIGN FIRM:

Bodman Design, Charlotte,

North Carolina

ART DIRECTOR/

DESIGNER/ILLUSTRATOR:

Catherine Bodman

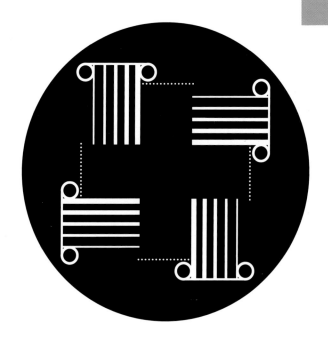

Symbol for development

campaign.

DESIGN FIRM:

Peter Nuhn/Graphic Design,

Stony Creek, Connecticut

DESIGNER: Peter Nuhn

Logo for the Davidson

Communities housing

development.

DESIGN FIRM:

Mires Design, Inc., San

Diego, California

ART DIRECTOR: Scott Mires

DESIGNER: Catherine Sachs

ILLUSTRATOR: Miguel Perez

MILANO

AT EASTLAKE GREENS

DESIGN FIRM:

Communication Arts,

Boulder, Colorado

ART DIRECTOR:

Richard Foy

DESIGNER:

Patricia Van Hook

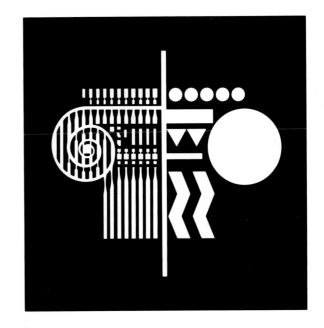

Logo for a blood analysis

machine.

DESIGN FIRM:

The Stephenz Group, San

Jose, California

CREATIVE DIRECTOR:

Stephanie Paulson

ART DIRECTORS:

Stephanie Paulson, Phillip

Kim

DESIGNER: Phillip Kim

Bio-Rad Laboratories (Medical Technology)

DESIGN FIRM:

Jacobson Design, Inc., New

York, New York

ART DIRECTOR/DESIGNER:

Clive Jacobson

DESIGN FIRM:

Ogdemli/Feldman Design,

North Hollywood, California

ART DIRECTOR/DESIGNER:

Shan Ogdemli

COMPUTER PRODUCTION:

Jim Venezia

Azalea Restaurant

DESIGN FIRM:

Sasaki Design Studio,

Seattle, Washington

ART DIRECTORS:

Yutaka K. Sasaki,

A. Kikutake Family

DESIGNER/ILLUSTRATOR:

Yutaka K. Sasaki

Bali Golf and Racquet Club

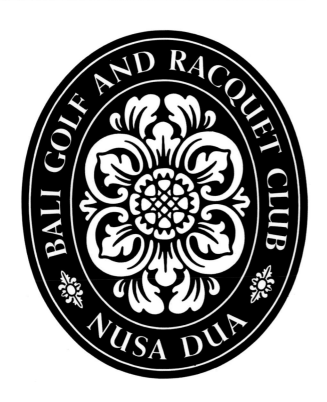

DESIGN FIRM:

Gerard Huerta Design, Inc.,

Southport, Connecticut

ART DIRECTOR: Peter Katz

DESIGNERS: Peter Katz,

Gerard Huerta

ILLUSTRATOR:

Gerard Huerta

Series of promotional pictograms.

DESIGN FIRM:

The Rockey Company, Seattle, Washington

ART DIRECTOR/DESIGNER:

Suzette K. LaPlant

ILLUSTRATOR: John Fretz

Port Blakely (Planned Community)

92

Promotional rubber stamp
series.
DESIGN FIRM:
Hirshorn-Zuckerman
Design Group, Rockville,
Maryland
ART DIRECTOR/
DESIGNER/ILLUSTRATOR:
John Gallagher

Hirshorn-Zuckerman Design Group

DESIGN FIRM:

Coulter Design, New

Britain, Connecticut

DESIGNER: Shawn Coulter

Dancing Bird Bistro (Restaurant)

DESIGN FIRM:

Pennebaker Design,

Houston, Texas

ART DIRECTOR/

DESIGNER/ILLUSTRATOR:

Jeffrey McKay

St. Pius Paul Festival & Dance

Pre-natal substance-abuse

program.

DESIGN FIRM:

Tackett-Barbaria Design,

Sacramento, California

ART DIRECTOR/

DESIGNER/ILLUSTRATOR:

Steve Barbaria

Options for Recovery

DESIGN FIRM:

Joe Duffy Design, Inc.,

Minneapolis, Minneapolis

ART DIRECTOR/DESIGNER:

Joe Duffy

ILLUSTRATORS: Joe Duffy,

Lynn Schulte

Minneapolis Public Library

DESIGN FIRM:

Art Chantry Design, Seattle,

Washington

ART DIRECTOR/DESIGNER:

Art Chantry

Screen print and product

(mostly T-shirts)

manufacturer.

DESIGN FIRM:

Art Chantry Design, Seattle,

Washington

ART DIRECTOR/DESIGNER:

Art Chantry

Post-Industrial Stress & Design

Logo for DeKuyper

volleyball series.

DESIGN FIRM: Segura, Inc.,

Chicago, Illinois

ART DIRECTOR/

DESIGNER/ILLUSTRATOR:

Carlos Segura

DESIGN FIRM:

C.S. Anderson Design

Company, Minneapolis,

Minneapolis

ART DIRECTORS/

DESIGNERS: C.S. Anderson,

Haley Johnson

ILLUSTRATORS:

Haley Johnson, Randall

Dahlk

Fossil (Watches)

DESIGNER/ILLUSTRATOR:

Patty O'Leary, Somerville,

Massachusetts

DESIGN FIRM:

Love Packaging Group,

Wichita, Kansas

ART DIRECTOR/

DESIGNER/ILLUSTRATOR:

Tracy Holdeman

Logo for festival held in
Little Chute, Wisconsin.

DESIGN FIRM:

Directions, Inc., Neenah,
Wisconsin

ART DIRECTOR/DESIGNER:

Lori Daun

DESIGN FIRM:

In 2 Print Graphics,
Brooklyn, New York

ART DIRECTOR/

DESIGNER/ILLUSTRATOR:

Dennis Clouse

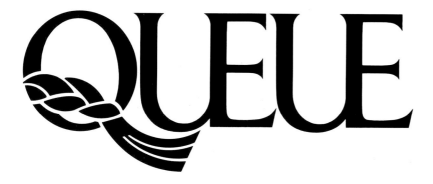

AGENCY:

Young & Rubicam, Inc.,

Detroit , Michigan

ART DIRECTOR/

DESIGNER/ILLUSTRATOR:

Steve Noxon

P U M P

R E C O R D S

Rap music label.

DESIGN FIRM:

Kimberly Baer Design

Associates, Venice,

California

ART DIRECTOR:

Kimberly Baer

DESIGNER/ILLUSTRATOR:

Elizabeth Burrill

Raul Varela

ART DIRECTOR/

DESIGNER/ILLUSTRATOR:

Raul Varela, Lake Charles,

Louisiana

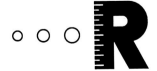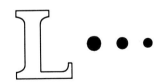

DESIGN FIRM:

Zida Borcich Letterpress,

Fort Bragg, California

ART DIRECTOR/DESIGNER:

Zida Borcich

ILLUSTRATOR:

Ludwig Enders

Daniel Corporation (Real Estate Development)

Golf and residential

community.

DESIGN FIRM:

Design Productions,

Birmingham, Alabama

CREATIVE DIRECTOR:

Stephanie Holland

ART DIRECTORS:

Bunny Chew, Chad

Bottcher, Ellen Strickland

ILLUSTRATOR: Jack Molloy

LETTERER: Elaine Dillard

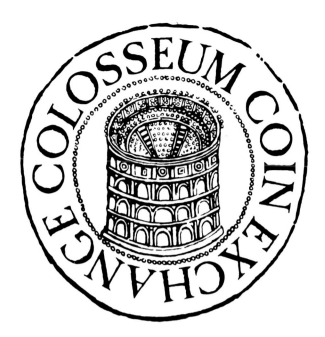

ART DIRECTOR/DESIGNER:

Steven Brower, New York,

New York

Thomas Neville Graphic Design

ART DIRECTOR/DESIGNER:

Thomas Neville, Newton

Upper Falls, Massachusetts

DESIGN FIRM:

Mars & Roz,

Seattle, Washington

ART DIRECTOR:

Roselynne Duavit-Pasion

DESIGNERS:

Marylin Esguerra,

Yutaka K. Sasaki

ILLUSTRATOR:

Yutaka K. Sasaki

Pre-natal care program.

DESIGN FIRM:

Richards & Swensen, Inc.,

Salt Lake City, Utah

ART DIRECTOR/

DESIGNER/ILLUSTRATOR:

William Swensen

Step One School

Non-profit pre-school.

DESIGN FIRM:

William Bevis Design,

Berkeley, California

ART DIRECTOR/DESIGNER:

Bill Bevis

ILLUSTRATOR: Tiana Seka

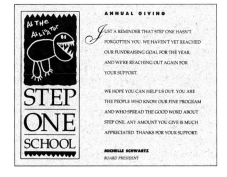

ANNUAL GIVING

*J*UST A REMINDER THAT STEP ONE HASN'T
FORGOTTEN YOU. WE HAVEN'T YET REACHED
OUR FUNDRAISING GOAL FOR THE YEAR,
AND WE'RE REACHING OUT AGAIN FOR
YOUR SUPPORT.

WE HOPE YOU CAN HELP US OUT. YOU ARE
THE PEOPLE WHO KNOW OUR FINE PROGRAM
AND WHO SPREAD THE GOOD WORD ABOUT
STEP ONE. ANY AMOUNT YOU GIVE IS MUCH
APPRECIATED. THANKS FOR YOUR SUPPORT.

MICHELLE SCHWARTZ
BOARD PRESIDENT

DESIGN FIRM:

Sandstrom Design, Portland,

Oregon

ART DIRECTOR/DESIGNER:

Steven Sandstrom

ILLUSTRATOR:

George Cheney

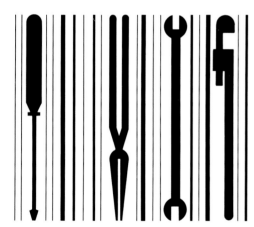

Software for barcoding

equipment to prevent loss

or theft.

DESIGN FIRM:

The Parker Group,

Chicago, Illinois

ART DIRECTOR:

Rex Parker

DESIGNER/ILLUSTRATOR:

Cathy Pawlowski

Robert Neumann Photography

DESIGN FIRM: True North,

Grand Rapids, Michigan

ART DIRECTOR/DESIGNER:

Tim Powers

Maxus Energy Corporation

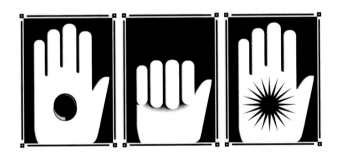

Symbol for employees

shareholding & investment

plan.

DESIGN FIRM:

Arday Design, DeSoto,

Texas

ART DIRECTOR/

DESIGNER/ILLUSTRATOR:

Don Arday

Logo for corporate travel

incentive program.

DESIGN FIRM:

Mires Design, Inc., San

Diego, California

ART DIRECTOR: Scott Mires

DESIGNER/ILLUSTRATOR:

Miguel Perez

A company that bronzes

baby shoes.

DESIGN FIRM:

Sullivan Perkins, Dallas,

Texas

ART DIRECTOR/DESIGNER:

Art Garcia

Bronze Me Baby

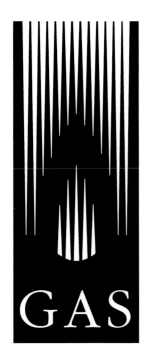

DESIGN FIRM:

Eric Woo Design, Inc.,

Honolulu, Hawaii

ART DIRECTOR/DESIGNER:

Eric Woo

PRI Gas Company

DESIGN FIRM: Tharp Did It,

Los Gatos, California

ART DIRECTOR:

Rick Tharp

DESIGNERS:

Jean Mogannam,

Rick Tharp

Bakeries By The Bay

A lending institution for

insurance premium

financing.

DESIGN FIRM:

Briley & Stables Creative,

Richardson, Texas

ART DIRECTOR/DESIGNER:

Ron Head

CCM Marketing (Marketing/Advertising)

DESIGN FIRM:

Emerson Wajdowicz

Studios, Inc., New York,

New York

ART DIRECTOR:

Jurek Wajdowicz

DESIGNER: Lisa LaRochelle

110

DESIGN FIRM:

United Pacific, Los Angeles,

California

DESIGNER: Wen Ping Hsiao

DESIGN FIRM:

Farkas Graphic Design,

Santa Rosa, California

ART DIRECTOR/DESIGNER:

Sandra Farkas

Logo for the council's 1993 San Antonio convention.

DESIGN FIRM:

Johnson Design Group, Inc., Falls Church, Virginia

ART DIRECTOR/ DESIGNER/ILLUSTRATOR:

Norasack Pathammavong

Council for Exceptional Children

ART DIRECTOR/DESIGNER:

Mark Palmer, Palm Desert, California

PRODUCTION: Curtis Palmer

Desert Rug Crafters

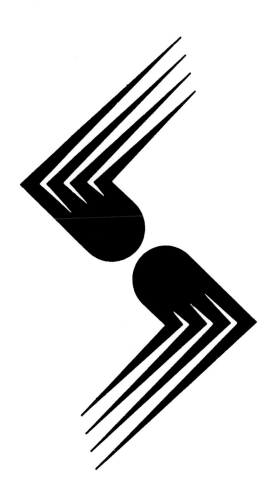

Company that disposes of
waste with a process
involving colliding
molecules.
DESIGN FIRM:
Eisenberg and Associates,
Dallas, Texas
ART DIRECTOR/DESIGNER:
Saul Torres
ILLUSTRATOR:
Garry Williams

Symbol for new medical-
product division.
DESIGN FIRM:
Firehouse Design Team,
Cincinnati, Ohio
ART DIRECTOR/DESIGNER:
Robert Probst

Laser Centers of America (Hospital Consultant/Service)

Breeder and trainer of
quarter horses.
DESIGN FIRM:
The Weller Institute for the
Cure of Design, Inc., Park
City, Utah
ART DIRECTOR/
DESIGNER/ILLUSTRATOR:
Don Weller

Design firm/cutting horse
ranch.
DESIGN FIRM:
The Weller Institute for the
Cure of Design, Inc., Park
City, Utah
ART DIRECTOR/
DESIGNER/ILLUSTRATOR:
Don Weller

Scott Mayeda (Graphic Design)

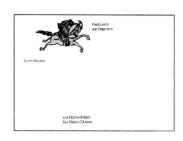

DESIGN FIRM:

Scott Mayeda, Freelance

Art Director, San Diego,

California

ART DIRECTOR/DESIGNER:

Scott Mayeda

Hammons Equestrian Center

DESIGN FIRM:

Sibley/Peteet Design,

Dallas, Texas

ART DIRECTOR/

DESIGNER/ILLUSTRATOR:

Julia Albanesi

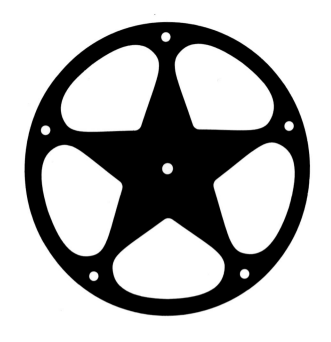

Film library at Southern

Methodist University.

DESIGN FIRM:

Eisenberg and Associates,

Dallas, Texas

ART DIRECTOR/DESIGNER:

Lee Collison

ILLUSTRATOR:

Michael Yancey

AGENCY:

Corn Fed Advertising,

Shaker Heights, Ohio

ART DIRECTOR/

DESIGNER/ILLUSTRATOR:

Debbie Klonk

Corn Fed Advertising

Counseling facility at St.

Vincent Health Center.

DESIGN FIRM:

Fritts & Hanna, Erie,

Pennsylvania

ART DIRECTOR:

William Hanna

DESIGNER:

April Hannah Tompkins

THE COUNSELING CENTER

HALIFAX

Logo for a seminar in   Dallas, Texas

Halifax, Nova Scotia   ART DIRECTOR: Tom Hair

DESIGN FIRM: DESIGNER: Jim Foley

Tom Hair Marketing Design,

117

Logos for fashion columns.

DESIGN FIRM:

The Columbus Dispatch,

Columbus, Ohio

ART DIRECTOR/DESIGNER:

Scott Minister

Logo for a sports medicine

infomercial.

DESIGN FIRM:

Janet + Judy Design

Associates, Inc., South

Norwalk, Connecticut

ART DIRECTOR:

Judy Rosenfeld

DESIGNERS:

Judy Rosenfeld, Janet

Scabrini

Yonchenko Communications

118

Video production company that produces 30-second spots.

DESIGN FIRM: "Fresh Paint", Versailles, Kentucky

ART DIRECTOR

DESIGNER/ILLUSTRATOR:

Stephen S. Sawyer

City of New Bern

Logo used to promote tourism.

DESIGN FIRM:

Buchanan Design, Richmond, Virginia

ART DIRECTOR/DESIGNER:

Margaret Buchanan

ILLUSTRATORS:

Margaret Buchanan, Les Derby

NEW BERN

The Colonial Capital Of North Carolina

Lion's Paw Antiques (Antique Shop)

AGENCY: Ogilvy & Mather

DESIGN FIRM:

Ken Shafer Design, Seattle,

Washington

ART DIRECTOR:

Chuck Pennington

DESIGNER/ILLUSTRATOR:

Ken Shafer

Police-sponsored event to

combat auto theft.

AGENCY:

Southland Advertising,

West Palm Beach, Florida

ART DIRECTOR/DESIGNER:

Rob Silio

Lock Out Crime

120

Logo commemorating the
25th anniversary of the
University's Meadows
Museum.
DESIGN FIRM:
Eisenberg and Associates,
Dallas, Texas
ART DIRECTOR/
DESIGNER/ILLUSTRATOR:
Bruce Wynne-Jones

DESIGNER: Janae Berry,
Greencastle, Indiana
ILLUSTRATOR:
Scott Johnson/Dean
Johnson Design, Inc.

Brackney's Men's Store

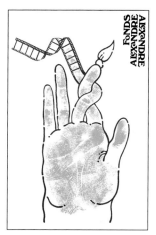

Logo for a collection of film and art-exhibition posters.

DESIGN FIRM:

Sommese Design, State College, Pennsylvania

ART DIRECTOR/

DESIGNER/ILLUSTRATOR:

Lanny Sommese

An independent food consultant who assists restaurant chains in menu planning, new recipes, and overall theme concepts.

DESIGN FIRM:

Ludwig Design, Kansas City, Missouri

DESIGNER/ILLUSTRATOR:

Kelly Ludwig

Rebeka Czufin

Chandler Illustration/Design

ART DIRECTOR/

DESIGNER/ILLUSTRATOR:

Roger Chandler, LaJolla,

California

Sweet Endings

A coffee house and dessert

shop.

DESIGN FIRM:

Cindy Slayton Creative,

Irving, Texas

CREATIVE DIRECTOR:

Cindy Slayton

123

Gecco (Computer Manufacturer)

DESIGN FIRM:

Smit Ghormley Lofgreen

Design, Phoenix, Arizona

DESIGNER: Art Lofgreen

The Jason Project

Symbol for the 1991

Galapagos expedition

sponsored by EDS

Corporate Communications.

ART DIRECTOR/

DESIGNER/ILLUSTRATOR:

Gary Daniels/EDS

Corporate Communications

Product symbol for a

computer mouse.

DESIGN FIRM:

Wen Ping Hsiao Design/Los

Angeles, Calabasas,

California

DESIGNER/ILLUSTRATOR:

Wen Ping Hsiao

AGENCY: Bozell, Inc.,

Minneapolis, Minneapolis

CREATIVE DIRECTOR:

Bert Gardner

ART DIRECTOR/

ILLUSTRATOR:

Steve Mitchell

Edith Davis Acupuncture

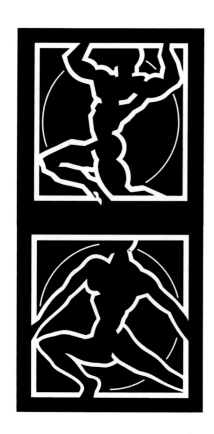

DESIGN FIRM:

Robert Domenz Design,

Elk Grove , illinois

ART DIRECTOR/

DESIGNER/ILLUSTRATOR:

Robert Domenz

126

DESIGN FIRM:

Battista Design, Boston,

Massachusetts

ART DIRECTOR/DESIGNER:

John Battista

ILLUSTRATORS:

John Battista, James Kraus

Baltimore City Commission for Women

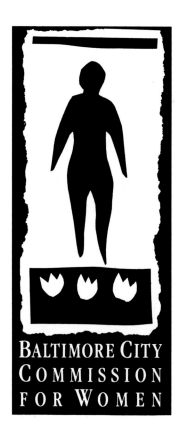

DESIGN FIRM:

Design and Graphics, DHCD,

Baltimore, Maryland

ART DIRECTOR/DESIGNER:

Gigi Moore

TYPOGRAPHY: Leslie Flax

A dry teen nightclub.

DESIGNER:

Michele P. Comas,

Brooklyn, New York

DESIGN FIRM:

Joe Pinciotti/Designer,

Toledo, Ohio

ART DIRECTOR/DESIGNER:

Joe Pinciotti

Jim Rohman (Photographer)

128

DESIGN FIRM:

Principia Graphica,

Portland, Oregon

ART DIRECTOR:

Robin Rickabaugh

ART DIRECTOR:

Heidi Rickabaugh

DESIGNERS: Jon Olsen,

Robin Rickabaugh

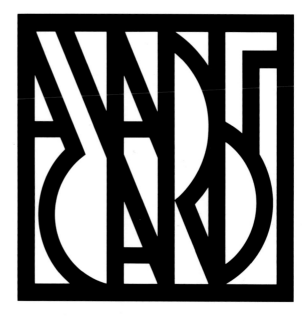

DESIGN FIRM: W.S. Design,

Sausalito, California

DESIGNER:

Wayne Sakamoto

DESIGN FIRM:

Smit Ghormley Lofgreen

Design, Phoenix, Arizona

DESIGNER: Art Lofgreen

bee jardin

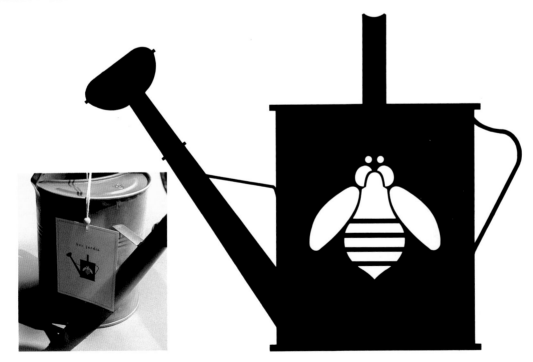

Company that specializes in decorative and hand-painted garden cans.

DESIGN FIRM: DESIGN!, Dalton, Georgia

ART DIRECTOR: Russ Ramage

DESIGNER: Sheryl Fendley

ILLUSTRATORS: Russ Ramage, Sheryl Fendley

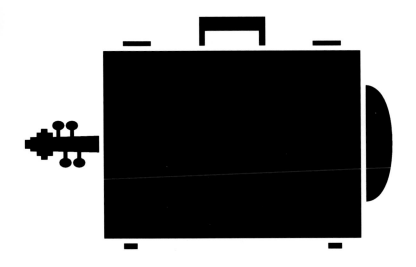

A corporate fundraising group for the Dallas Symphony.

DESIGN FIRM:

Tom Lout and Company, Inc., Dallas, Texas

ART DIRECTOR/DESIGNER:

Tom Lout

Corporate Partners

DESIGN FIRM:

Love Packaging Group, Wichita, Kansas

ART DIRECTOR/ DESIGNER/ILLUSTRATOR:

Tracy Holdeman

Holdeman's Total Lawn Care

HOLDEMAN'S TOTAL LAWN CARE SERVICE

TRIMMING

CLIPPING

MOWING

EDGING

FERTILIZING

KIM HOLDEMAN
☎ 904 327 4612
6000 DORAN RD.
WALNUTHILL FL
32568

HOMELAND

THE HOMELAND PROJECT

Documentary film about

rebuilding Russia.

DESIGN FIRM:

Bouthillier Design

Associates, Inc., Plymouth,

Massachusetts

ART DIRECTOR/

DESIGNER/ILLUSTRATOR:

Lans Bouthillier

Hamilton County Convention and Visitors Bureau (Tourism)

DESIGN FIRM: Antenna,

Indianapolis, Indiana

DESIGNERS: James Sholly,

Laura Lacy-Sholly

HAMILTON
·COUNTY·
INDIANA

TOWNS &
COUNTRY

DESIGN FIRM:

Lane/Morris, Inc.,

Wilmington, Delaware

DESIGNER/ILLUSTRATOR:

Mark Bartman

DESIGN FIRM:

Susanna Ronner Graphic

Design, Bearsville, New

York

DESIGNER/ILLUSTRATOR:

Susanna Ronner

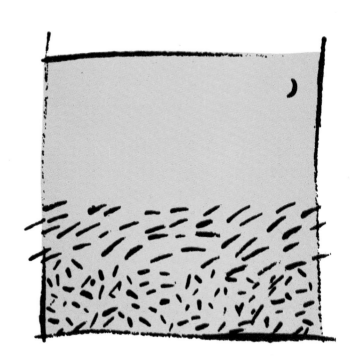

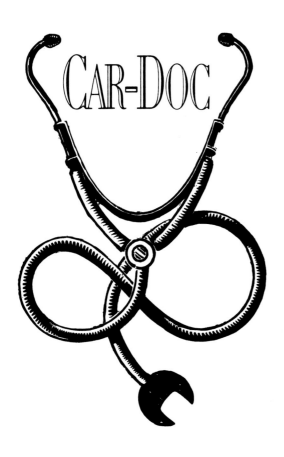

A physician who restores

classic automobiles.

DESIGN FIRM:

Nichols-Dezenhall

Communications

Management Group,

Evanston, Illinois

ART DIRECTOR/DESIGNER:

Kathleen W. Herring

ILLUSTRATOR:

Stuart Armstrong

Logo for CD cover.

DESIGN FIRM:

Margo Chase Design, Los

Angeles, California

DESIGNER/ILLUSTRATOR:

Margo Chase

Keith Richards (Music)

DESIGN FIRM:

Tom Fowler, Inc., Stamford,

Connecticut

ART DIRECTOR/

DESIGNER/ILLUSTRATOR:

Thomas G. Fowler

Hudson Bar and Books

DESIGNER: Tim Gormley,

Fairfield, Connecticuty

Gormley Design

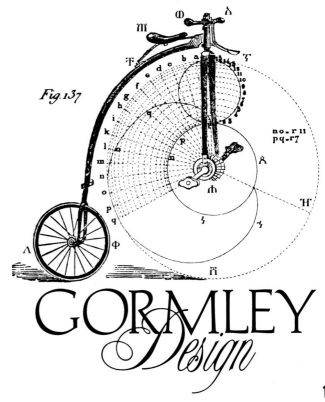

Logo for children's festivals

sponsored by local zoos.

DESIGN FIRM:

Lorel Marketing Group, Inc.,

King of Prussia, Pennsylvania

ART DIRECTOR:

Scott Laserow

DESIGNER/ILLUSTRATOR:

Sue Buchholtz Naylor

DESIGNER/ILLUSTRATOR:

Jennifer Hewitson, Cardiff,

California

DESIGN FIRM:

Smit Ghormley Lofgreen,

Phoenix, Arizona

DESIGNER: Art Lofgreen

Washington Street Bar and Grill

DESIGN FIRM:

Grant Associates, Boston,

Massachusetts

ART DIRECTOR/

DESIGNER/ILLUSTRATOR:

Craig Grant

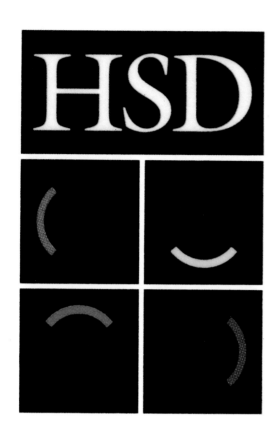

ART DIRECTOR/

DESIGNER/ILLUSTRATOR:

Jodie Stowe, Menlo Park,

California

Shin Sun (Frozen Food)

Non-profit company that
produces frozen entrees
based on Korean recipes;
formed to provide an
alternative to "sweat shop"
employment for Korean
women in San Francisco.

DESIGN FIRM:

Longenecker Design,

Aptos, California

ART DIRECTOR:

Laurie Longenecker

DESIGNERS: Irene Morris,

Laurie Longenecker

DESIGN FIRM: Art Factory,

Elm Grove, Wisconsin

ART DIRECTOR/DESIGNER:

Jim Wagner

WEST ◆ BEND
G A L L E R Y
O F ◆ F I N E ◆ A R T S
300 SOUTH SIXTH AVE
WEST BEND, WI 53095
PHONE (414) 334-9638

DESIGN FIRM:

Ted Bertz Design, Inc.,

Middletown, Connecticut

ART DIRECTORS:

Ted Bertz, Keri Beaton

ILLUSTRATOR: Keri Beaton

Stephen Bank (Psychotherapy)

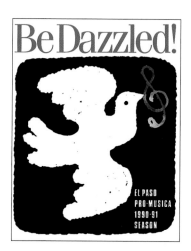

A choral/instrumental

group.

AGENCY:

Mithoff Advertising Inc.,

El Paso, Texas

ART DIRECTOR/

DESIGNER/ILLUSTRATOR:

Clive Cochran

Logo designed to identify

products manufactured

exclusively with wool grown

in the U.S.

AGENCY:

Evan Scott Advertising,

New York, New York

CREATIVE DIRECTOR:

Evan Gross

ART DIRECTOR: Jodi Crupi

AMERICAN WOOL

DESIGN FIRM:

Cole-Zielanski Design,

Frostburg, Maryland

ART DIRECTOR/

DESIGNER/ILLUSTRATOR:

Trudy Cole-Zielanski

LARRY PAO DESIGN : 1991 · CELEBRATING THE 1ST DECADE

Logo commemorating

firm's 10th anniversary.

DESIGN FIRM:

Larry Pao Design, Inc.,

Costa Mesa, California

ART DIRECTORS:

Michael Dula, Larry Pao

DESIGNER/ILLUSTRATOR:

Michael Dula

Larry Pao Design, Inc.

Series of promotional icons.

DESIGN FIRM:

Corey McPherson Nash,

Watertown, Massachusetts

ART DIRECTOR: Tom Corey

ILLUSTRATOR:

Anthony Russo

DESIGNER: Tammy Radmer

Turner Network Television

SIMON

An educational training

program.

DESIGN FIRM: Wood Design,

New York, New York

DESIGNER/ILLUSTRATOR:

Tom Wood

Logo for an annual civic

event held to raise funds for

nonprofit organizations.

DESIGN FIRM:

Hilary Hudgens Design,

Dallas, Texas

ART DIRECTOR:

Hilary Hudgens

DESIGNER/ILLUSTRATOR:

Greg Morgan

DESIGN FIRM:

Peterson & Company,

Dallas, Texas

ART DIRECTOR:

Scott Paramski

DESIGNERS:

Scott Paramski, Bryan L.

Peterson

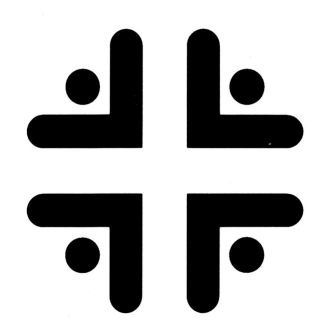

Plano Children's Medical Clinic

DESIGN FIRM:

Peterson & Company,

Dallas, Texas

ART DIRECTOR:

Bryan L. Peterson

DESIGNER: Scott Feaster

Concrete Productions (Film)

DESIGN FIRM: Segura, Inc.,

Chicago, Illinois

ART DIRECTOR/

DESIGNER/ILLUSTRATOR:

Carlos Segura

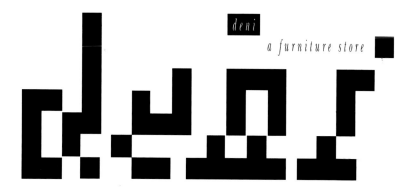

deni

a furniture store

ART DIRECTOR/

DESIGNER/ILLUSTRATOR:

Craig Bissell, Kansas City,

Missouri

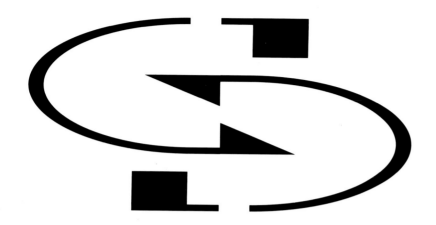

DESIGN FIRM:

Palmquist & Palmquist

Design, Bozeman, Montana

ART DIRECTORS:

Kurt and Denise Palmquist

DESIGNER/ILLUSTRATOR:

Kurt Palmquist

C/C Interior Design Inc.

DESIGN FIRM:

Linschoten & Associates,

Honolulu, Hawaii

ART DIRECTOR/DESIGNER:

Bud Linschoten

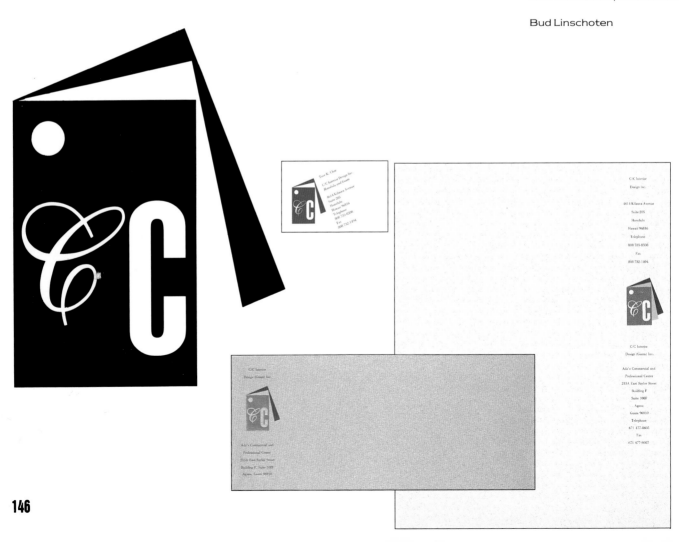

DESIGN FIRM:

Levinson Creative,

Brooklyn, New York

DESIGNER: Peter Levinson

Producer of radio programs

and publications.

DESIGN FIRM:

Frank D'Astolfo Design,

New York, New York

ART DIRECTOR/DESIGNER:

Frank D'Astolfo

XYZ Productions (Radio)

Series of logos for the

varieties of coffee served.

DESIGN FIRM:

96 Eyes Design, Pittsburgh,

Pennsylvania

ART DIRECTORS/

DESIGNERS/

ILLUSTRATORS:

Michael Lotenero, Richard

Bach

ETHIOPIAN YRGACHEFFE

BEEHIVE BLEND

KENYA KENYA

GUATEMALA

KENYA DECAF

MOCHA JAVA

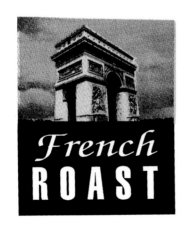

French ROAST

ITALIAN ROAST

HOGAN'S MARKET

DESIGN FIRM:

Hornall Anderson Design

Works, Seattle, Washington

ART DIRECTORS:

Jack Anderson, Julia LaPine

DESIGNERS:

Jack Anderson, Julia

LaPine, Denise Weir, Lian Ng

ILLUSTRATOR: Larry Jost

COPYWRITER:

Bill Bailey Carter

DESIGN FIRM:

Image Design, Nashville,

Tennessee

ART DIRECTOR/DESIGNER:

Robert Froedge

Cheesecakes & Other Delights, Inc.

CHEESECAKES
& OTHER DELIGHTS
INCORPORATED

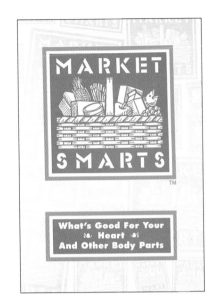

A program of supermarket tours arranged by a dietician.

DESIGN FIRM: Dean Wilhite Design Company, Oklahoma City, Oklahoma

ART DIRECTOR/ DESIGNER/ ILLUSTRATOR: Dean Wilhite

COPYWRITER: Elizabeth Laurent/Laurent & Company

A company in El Salvador that exports fresh-frozen shrimp.

DESIGN FIRM: Eric Woo Design, Inc., Honolulu, Hawaii

ART DIRECTOR/ DESIGNER/ILLUSTRATOR: Eric Woo

PACIFIC FIESTA

DESIGN FIRM:

Tom Lout and Company,

Inc., Dallas, Texas

ART DIRECTOR/DESIGNER:

Tom Lout

A fun, food and

entertainment fair.

DESIGN FIRM:

Julia Tam Design, Palos

Verdes, California

ART DIRECTOR/DESIGNER:

Julia Chong Tam

ILLUSTRATOR: Karen Bell

DESIGN FIRM:

Mark Palmer Design, Palm

Desert, California

ART DIRECTOR/DESIGNER:

Mark Palmer

PRODUCTION: Curtis Palmer

Carr Communications

Logo for a charity fashion

show featuring local

celebrities and their pets.

DESIGN FIRM:

Ken Shafer Design

AGENCY:

Nordstrom Advertising,

Seattle, Washington

ART DIRECTOR/DESIGNER:

Ken Shafer

CREATIVE DIRECTOR:

Cheryl Zahniser/Nordstrom

Advertising

TUXES & TAILS

Tuxes & Tails

DESIGN FIRM: Pentagram,

New York, New York

ART DIRECTOR:

Woody Pirtle

DESIGNER:

Susan Hochbaum

A llama ranch and apparel

business.

DESIGN FIRM:

Palmquist & Palmquist

Design, Bozeman, Montana

ART DIRECTORS:

Denise and Kurt Palmquist

DESIGNER/ILLUSTRATOR:

Denise Palmquist

Llamas & Llooms

Gasmark, Inc.

A gas marketing and

pipeline company.

DESIGN FIRM:

Piland/Goodell, Inc.,

Houston, Texas

DESIGNER: Don Goodell

ILLUSTRATOR: Paul Hera

Chargo Printing, Inc.

DESIGN FIRM:

GrandPré and Whaley, Ltd.,

St. Paul, Minnesota

ART DIRECTOR/DESIGNER:

Kevin Whaley

Ethnic skin care salon.

DESIGN FIRM:

Image Design, Inc.,

Nashville, Tennessee

ART DIRECTOR/DESIGNER:

Howard Diehl

Logo for a Saint Patrick's

Day dance and fundraiser

for a local charity.

DESIGN FIRM:

Love Packaging Group,

Wichita, Kansas

ART DIRECTOR/

DESIGNER/ILLUSTRATOR:

Chris West

Emerald Ball

DESIGN FIRM:

Ogdemli/Feldman Design,

North Hollywood, California

ART DIRECTOR/

DESIGNER/ILLUSTRATOR:

Shan Ogdemli

DESIGN FIRM:

Bottega Design, Inc., Des

Plaines, Illinois

ART DIRECTOR/DESIGNER:

Deborah Doering

Overland Trading Co. (Footwear)

DESIGN FIRM:

Midnight Oil Studios, New

York, New York

ART DIRECTOR/

DESIGNER/ILLUSTRATOR:

Kathryn Klein

Swedish Eagle (Radio Disk Jockey)

DESIGN FIRM:

Aalvik Design, Whittier,

California

ART DIRECTOR/

DESIGNER/ILLUSTRATOR:

Ena Rocha Aalvik

Employee service campaign

promoting quality control.

DESIGN FIRM:

Hornall Anderson Design

Works, Seattle, Washington

ART DIRECTOR:

Jack Anderson

DESIGNERS:

Jack Anderson, David

Bates

Food Services of America

DESIGN FIRM:

Love Packaging Group,

Wichita, Kansas

ART DIRECTOR/

DESIGNER/ILLUSTRATOR:

Chris West

Impressions of Wichita (Printing)

159

DESIGN FIRM:

The Office of Reginald Wade

Richey, Denver , Colorado

ART DIRECTOR:

Reginald Wade Richey

DESIGNER/ILLUSTRATOR:

Karl Hirschmann

Skin'N'Bones

DESIGN FIRM:

Jerman Design
Incorporated, Salt Lake
City, Utah

ART DIRECTOR/DESIGNER:

Steven R. Jerman

Skin'N'Bones (Funk/Rock Band)

Festival sponsored by
Issaquah Chamber of
Commerce.

DESIGN FIRM:

Brickbottom Design Group,
Norwell, Massachusetts

ART DIRECTOR/DESIGNER:

Judith Moncrieff

Issaquah Salmon Days

DESIGN FIRM:

Brad Norr Design,

Minneapolis, Minneapolis

DESIGNER: Brad Norr

DESIGN FIRM:

Design Center, Minnetonka,

Minneapolis

ART DIRECTOR/DESIGNER:

Todd Spichke

Minko Construction Company

162

DESIGN FIRM:

Jon Henjum Design, Green

Bay, Wisconsin

ART DIRECTOR/DESIGNER:

Jon Henjum

Educational program
designed to expose Latino
and other schoolchildren to
the scientific, environmental
and cultural importance of
the oceans.

DESIGN FIRM:

Puccinelli Design, Santa

Barbara, California

ART DIRECTOR/

DESIGNER/ILLUSTRATOR:

Keith Puccinelli

Los Marineros
113 Harbor Way
Santa Barbara
California 93109
(805) 966-7107

Los Marineros

A division of the National
Association of Home
Builders, comprising four
groups of single-family
house builders administered
by one office.

DESIGN FIRM:
Arts & Letters, Ltd., Falls
Church, Virginia
ART DIRECTOR: Susan Eder
DESIGNER: Craig Dennis

DESIGNER:

Terri Russler-Deval, Ann
Arbor, Michigan

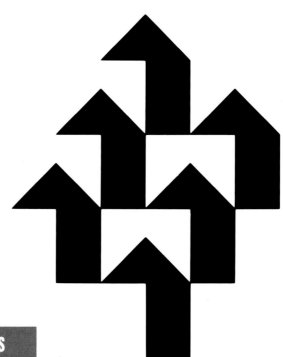

Daymond Building Products

164

Memphis Jewish Community Center

Symbol for a fundraising
drive to renovate and
update facilities.

DESIGN FIRM:

David Meyer Graphic Design
& Illustration, Memphis,
Tennessee

ART DIRECTOR/

DESIGNER/ILLUSTRATOR:

David Meyer

All Nations Nursery & Child Care

DESIGN FIRM: Quorum, Inc.,

Ann Arbor, Michigan

ART DIRECTOR:

Doug Hesseltine

DESIGNERS:

Rhonda DeMason, Christine

Golus

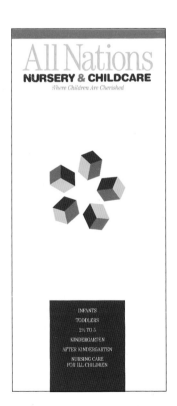

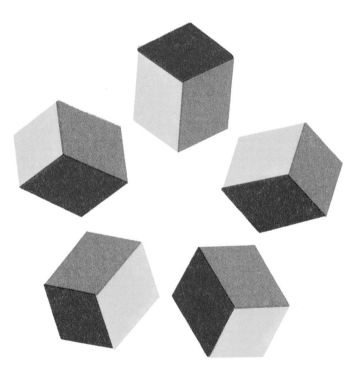

165

DESIGN FIRM:

Pictogram Studio,

Washington, DC

ART DIRECTOR:

Hien Nguyen

DESIGNERS: Hien Nguyen,

Stephanie Hooton

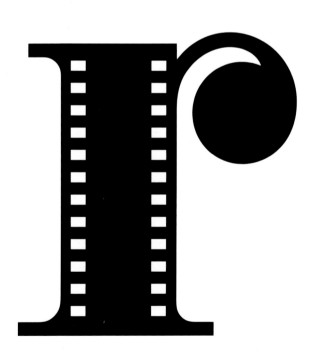

DESIGN FIRM:

Zust & Company, Cleveland,

Ohio

DESIGNER: Mark Zust

Peter Renerts Studio (Photographer)

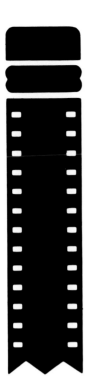

DESIGN FIRM:

Pfeiffer & Company,

St. Louis, Missouri

ART DIRECTOR/DESIGNER:

Renee Walsh

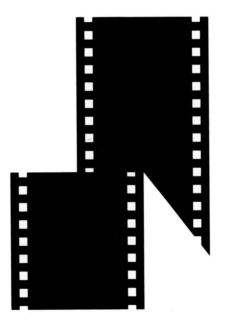

DESIGN FIRM:

Th'ng Design, Baton Rouge,

Louisiana

ART DIRECTOR/

DESIGNER/ILLUSTRATOR:

Charlie Th'ng

PRINTER:

Franklin Press, Inc.

Davison Production, Inc. (Film Producer)

DESIGN FIRM:

C.S. Anderson Design Co.,

Minneapolis, Minneapolis

ART DIRECTOR/

DESIGNER/ILLUSTRATOR:

Haley Johnson

DESIGN FIRM:

Bottega Design, Inc., Des

Plaines, Illinois

ART DIRECTOR:

Deborah Doering

DESIGNER: Susan Weller

Niles West High School Counseling Department

Logo for national
conference.
DESIGN FIRM:
Held & Diedrich Design,
Indianapolis, Indiana
ART DIRECTOR/
DESIGNER/ILLUSTRATOR:
Tim Gant

Symbol for copywriter Jane
Siegel.
DESIGN FIRM:
L.A. Graphics, Grand
Rapids, Michigan
ART DIRECTOR/
DESIGNER/ILLUSTRATOR:
Lynn Ayres-Strough

Creative Stuff

F R A U E N S H U H   D E V E L O P M E N T

DESIGN FIRM: CLX,

Minneapolis, Minneapolis

ART DIRECTOR/DESIGNER:

Peter Winecke

Frauenshuh Development (Commercial Property Development)

DESIGNER/ILLUSTRATOR:

Kevin Mason, Santa

Monica, California

Ramco Inc. (Contracting)

Consortium logo.

ART DIRECTOR:

Scott Greer/DCE Design,

University of Utah, Salt

Lake City, Utah

DESIGNER: Tadd Peterson

DESIGN FIRM:

England Design, Dayton,

Ohio

ART DIRECTOR/DESIGNER:

Michael England

MIKE ENGLAND
GRAPHIC DESIGN

513.434.5882

160.G
DEVONHURST
DRIVE

KETTERING
OHIO
45429

England Design

RAFN Company

Specializes in a partnership approach to commercial renovation, multi-unit residential construction, and interior tenant improvements.

DESIGN FIRM:
Hornall Anderson Design
Works, Seattle, Washington
ART DIRECTOR:
Jack Anderson
DESIGNER: Jack Anderson,
Jani Drewfs, David Bates

Modesto Junior College

Symbol for the college's
Little Theatre.
DESIGN FIRM:
Marcia Herrmann Design,
Modesto , California
DESIGNER/ILLUSTRATOR:
Marcia Herrmann

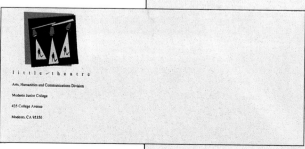

172

C A M E L B A C K
G O L F • C L U B

S C O T T S D A L E
A R I Z O N A

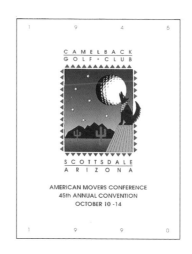

Logo for annual convention of the national association representing van lines, agents and independent household goods moving and storage companies.

DESIGN FIRM:

Steele Graphic Design, Annandale, Virginia

ART DIRECTORS:

Carolyn C. Steele, Bruce MacKechnie

DESIGNER/ILLUSTRATOR:

Carolyn C. Steele

Neighborhood restaurant that encourages patrons to exchange old maps for discounts. The maps are used as decoration.

DESIGNER/ILLUSTRATOR:

Rick Blasdell, York, Pennsylvania

Logo for photography
contest sponsored by the
publication.
DESIGN FIRM:
Morreal Graphic Design,
San Diego, California
DESIGNER:
Mary Lou Morreal

Product logo for a security
sensor used primarily for
the protection of paintings.
DESIGN FIRM:
GrandPré and Whaley, Ltd.,
St. Paul, Minnesota
ART DIRECTOR/DESIGNER:
Kevin Whaley

Theme logo for graphic arts
exposition.

DESIGN FIRM:

Salvato & Coe Associates,

Columbus, Ohio

ART DIRECTOR/DESIGNER:

Steve Gabor

Columbus Chamber of Commerce

Electronics for Imaging

Company involved in

prepress on the Macintosh.

DESIGN FIRM:

Woods & Woods, San

Francisco, California

ART DIRECTOR/DESIGNER:

Paul Woods

DESIGN FIRM:

Len Visual Design, Helena,

Montana

DESIGNER/ILLUSTRATOR:

Len Eckel

Sara Thompson Landscape Design

DESIGN FIRM:

Veronica Miller &

Associates, Haverford,

Pennsylvania

ART DIRECTOR/

DESIGNER/ILLUSTRATOR:

Veronica Miller

Symbol for a joint film
venture between Japan and
the U.S.
DESIGN FIRM:
Diane Kuntz Design, Inc.,
Santa Monica, California
ART DIRECTOR/DESIGNER:
Diane Kuntz

DESIGN FIRM:

Harriman Creative,

Minneapolis, Minneapolis

ART DIRECTOR/

DESIGNER/ILLUSTRATOR:

B.R. Harriman

Series of symbols used in

holiday invitation.

DESIGN FIRM:

Tom Fowler, Inc., Stamford,

Connecticut

ART DIRECTOR/

DESIGNER/ILLUSTRATOR:

Thomas G. Fowler

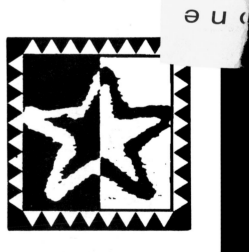

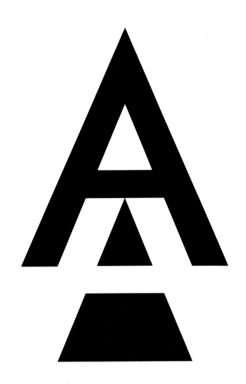

Advanced Surgical, Inc.

Designer of surgical instruments which can penetrate muscle through very small openings.

DESIGN FIRM:

Pentagram Design, New York, New York

AGENCY: Noonan Russo

ART DIRECTOR:

Woody Pirtle

DESIGNERS: Woody Pirtle, John Klotnia

Ulman Paper Bag Company

DESIGN FIRM:

Supon Design Group, Inc., Washington, DC

ART DIRECTOR/DESIGNER:

Supon Phornirunlit

180

First Colony (Coffee)

Logo for a new line of dark roast coffees.

AGENCY: Finnegan & Agee, Richmond, Virginia

CREATIVE DIRECTOR: Ed Jones

ART DIRECTOR: Jim Brock

ILLUSTRATOR: Scott Wright

ACCOUNT SUPERVISOR: Lisa Finnegan

East Jefferson General Hospital

Symbol for corporate health-education and screening/early detection program.

DESIGN FIRM:

The Graham Group, Lafayette, Louisiana

ART DIRECTOR/ DESIGNER/ILLUSTRATOR: Nancy Marcotte

Montana Street Café

DESIGN FIRM:

Murrie Lienhart Rysner &

Associates, Chicago, Illinois

ART DIRECTOR/

DESIGNER/ILLUSTRATOR:

Linda Voll

Promotional logo for the

1991 eclipse of the sun

observed in Mexico.

DESIGN FIRM:

Garza/Winter

Communications, Los

Angeles, California

DESIGNER: Agustin Garza

Mexican Board of Tourism

182

California Spring (Health & Beauty Products)

DESIGN FIRM:

Art Kilinski Design, San

Jose, California

ART DIRECTOR/

DESIGNER/ILLUSTRATOR:

Art Kilinski

DESIGN FIRM:

Hubbard and Hubbard

Design, Phoenix, Arizona

ART DIRECTOR/

DESIGNER/ILLUSTRATOR:

Ann Morton Hubbard

Body Sculpture Gym (Fitness)

Logo for company's United

Way campaign.

DESIGN FIRM:

Studio Dudeo, Minneapolis,

Minneapolis

ART DIRECTOR:

Debra Bistodeau

DESIGNER: Susan Serstock

Target Department Stores

Logos for an association of

art gallery owners.

DESIGN FIRM:

Sackett Design, San

Francisco, California

ART DIRECTOR/DESIGNER:

Mark Sackett

ILLUSTRATOR:

Chris Yaryan

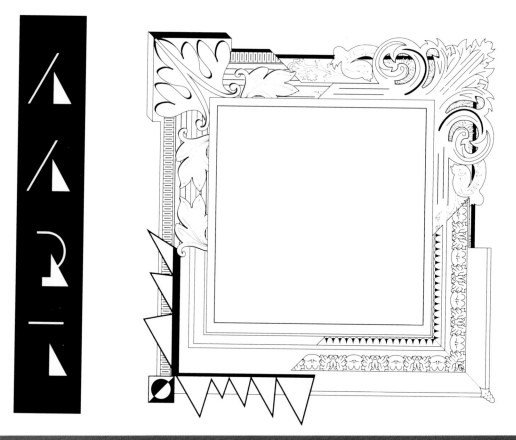

The AART Group

A ROCK OPERA

Logo for a production of a rock opera.

DESIGN FIRM:

Rives Carlberg, Houston, Texas

CREATIVE DIRECTOR:

Sherri Oldham

ART DIRECTOR/

DESIGNER/ILLUSTRATOR:

Jesus Felix

Alpha Furniture Restoration

DESIGN FIRM:

Kowalski Designworks,

Inc., Berkeley, California

ART DIRECTOR:

Stephen Kowalski

DESIGNERS:

Stephen Kowalski,

Christine McFarren

ALPHA
FURNITURE
RESTORATION

185

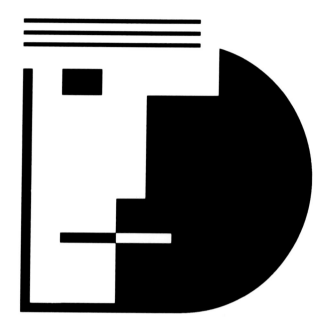

DESIGN FIRM:

McNulty & Company,

Montrose, California

ART DIRECTOR/DESIGNER:

Dan McNulty

PRODUCTION

REFINEMENT:

Jennifer Birkland

Voters for Choice

Logo for Voices for Choice

benefit concert.

DESIGN FIRM:

J. Gibson & Co.,

Washington, DC

ART DIRECTOR:

Gibby Edwards

DESIGNER:

Lisa M. Brzezniak

Logo for international
soccer matches organizing
committee.

DESIGN FIRM:

Pentagram Design, New

York, New York

ART DIRECTORS:

Michael Gericke, Woody

Pirtle

DESIGNERS:

Michael Gericke, James

Anderson

DESIGN FIRM:

C.S. Anderson Design Co.,

Minneapolis, Minneapolis

ART DIRECTOR/DESIGNER:

Charles S. Anderson

Spazio Institute (Developer)

Creative Directors
Design Directors
Art Directors
Designers

Illustrators
Typographers
Production Artists
Computer Artists